TWO LAKES
ふたつのみずうみ

This special edition in the *Laboratorium* series is an outcome of a collaboration between Hochschule Luzern – Technik & Architektur, Institut für Architektur (Lucerne University of Applied Sciences and Arts – Institute of Architecture) and Kyoto Institute of Technology – KYOTO Design Lab in the periode of 2018–2023.

Edited by

GEISSBÜHLER Dieter
KÄFERSTEIN Johannes
KIMURA Hiroyuki
KINOSHITA Masashiro
SUN BUSCHOR Mulan

Laboratorium Switzerland – Japan

TWO LAKES
ふたつのみずうみ

Lake Lucerne and Lake Biwa:
A Comparative Study on the Culture of Water

QUART

Hochschule Luzern – Technik & Architektur IAR
Kyoto Institute of Technology – KYOTO Design Lab

Photos by BECK Jürgen

LAKE LUCERNE – VIERWALDSTÄTTERSEE

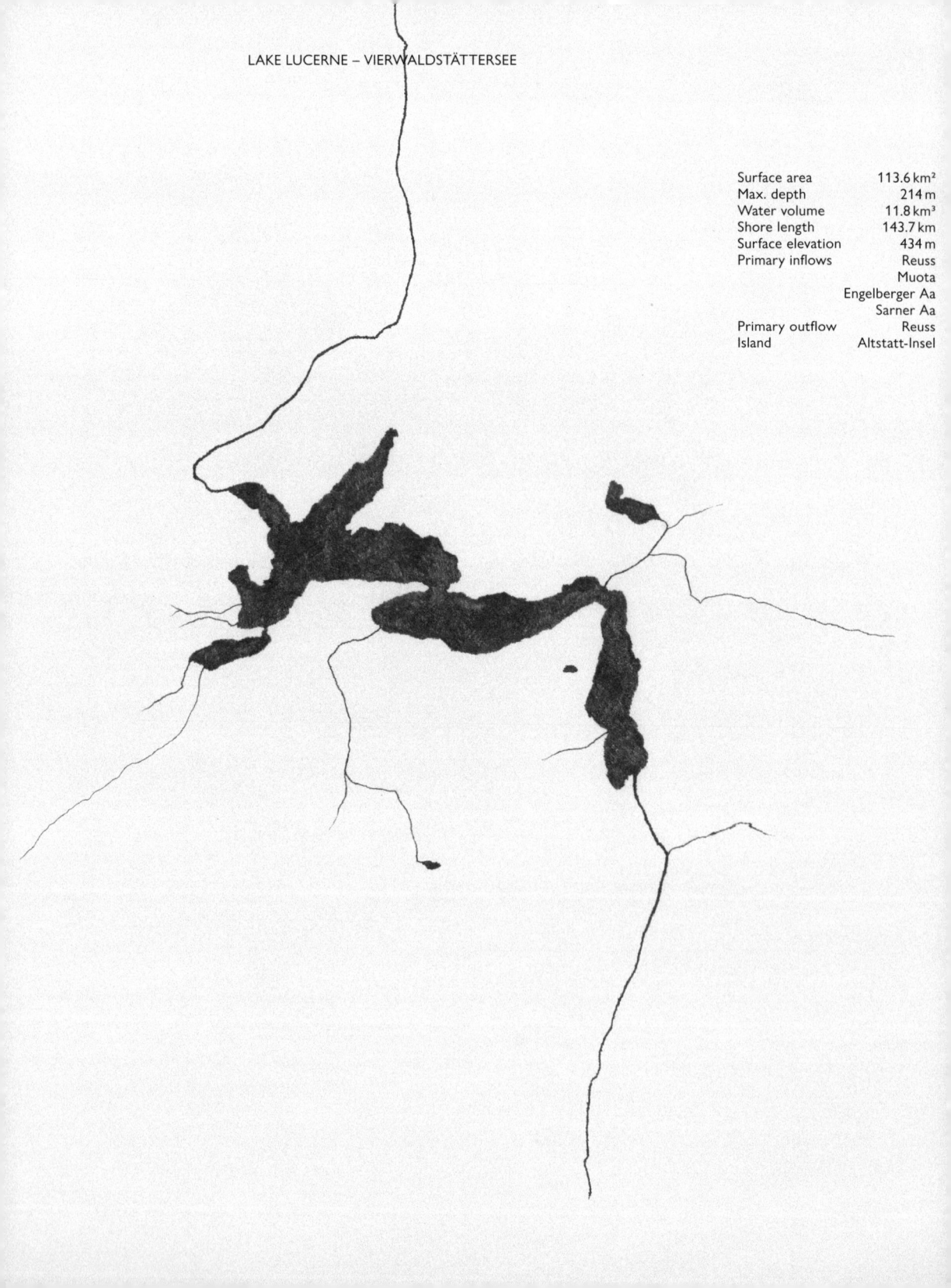

Surface area	113.6 km²
Max. depth	214 m
Water volume	11.8 km³
Shore length	143.7 km
Surface elevation	434 m
Primary inflows	Reuss
	Muota
	Engelberger Aa
	Sarner Aa
Primary outflow	Reuss
Island	Altstatt-Insel

LAKE BIWA – 琵琶湖

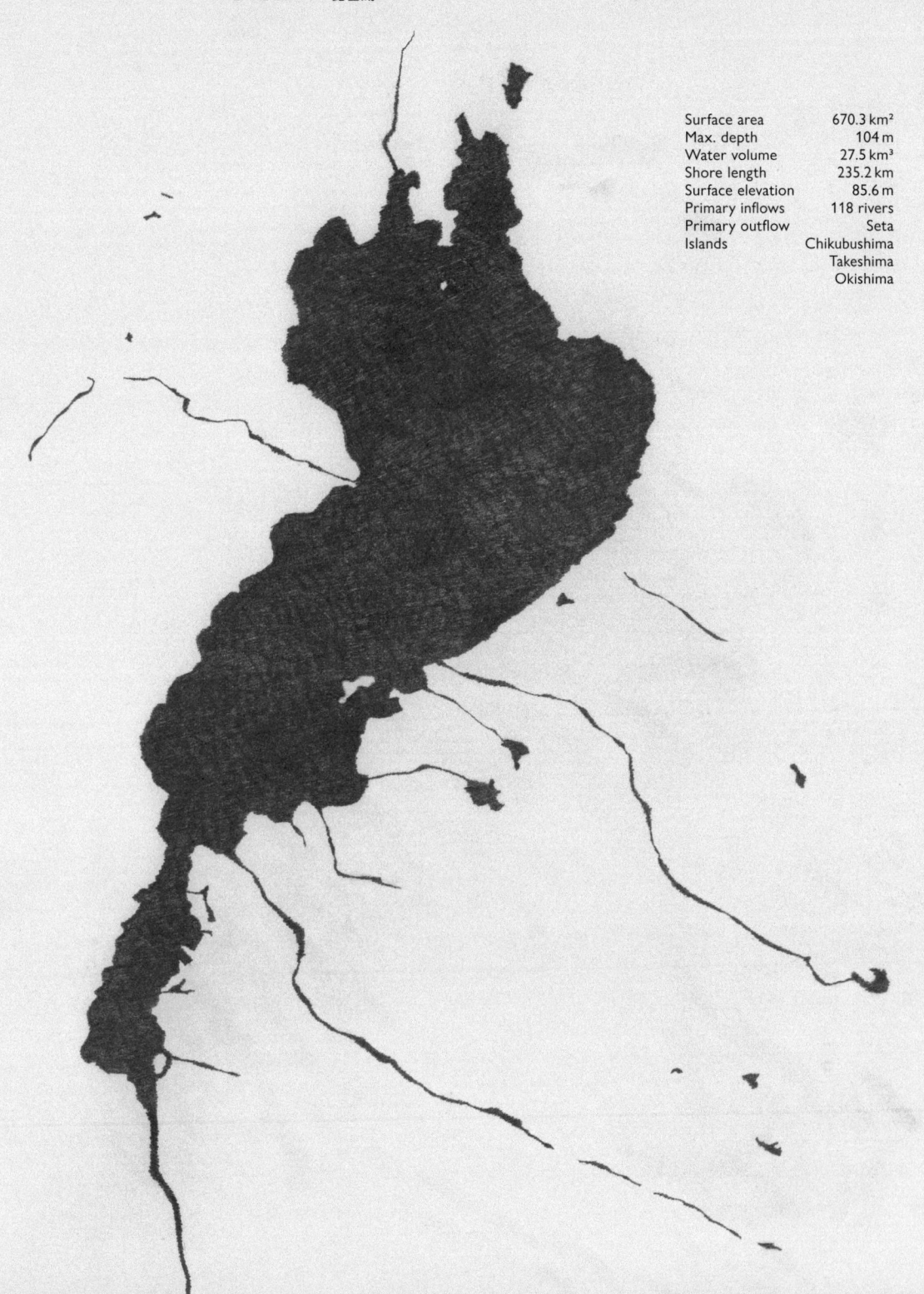

Surface area	670.3 km²
Max. depth	104 m
Water volume	27.5 km³
Shore length	235.2 km
Surface elevation	85.6 m
Primary inflows	118 rivers
Primary outflow	Seta
Islands	Chikubushima
	Takeshima
	Okishima

Photos by TAKANO Tomomi

TWO LAKES – TWO FRIENDS
ふたつのみずうみ – ふたりの友

KÄFERSTEIN Johannes

In 2018, the Institute of Architecture at the Lucerne School of Engineering and Architecture and the Kyoto Design Lab at the Kyoto Institute of Technology decided to run a joint five-year design programme with their master's studios. The mutual fascination for the respective architecture and culture was the cornerstone of this ten-semester open research programme. The common starting point for the research programme was neither the strongly developed timber construction tradition, which is comparable on many levels, nor the use of concrete, which has been developed to perfection in both countries, but two lakes. Water is the cornerstone of all life. The different relationships that people and societies have to water can offer the key to a culture – this was our hypothesis.

We used Lake Lucerne and Lake Biwa near Kyoto to embark upon a journey between the two worlds. The element of water proved to be both a mirror and a gateway. The repeated confrontations with our own and the other culture opened ways for us to understand the foreign, in which we recognised ourselves again and again. Symbolically, we pushed through the looking glass of nature and plunged into an initially uncertain depth. In order to understand, we began to systematically read, describe, draw, film and narrate the world we thought we saw and knew. We realised that we had to approach it with all the means at our disposal. In addition to the settlements, infrastructure, industrial uses, transport and tourism facilities that have developed over the centuries, the political and cultural dimensions of both lakes emerged and expanded. How can beauty, history and timelessness persist in an environment that is subject to unstoppable pressure from vested interests? How can we prevent a balance between landscape and settlement areas that has evolved over centuries from being constantly and irretrievably destroyed by urban sprawl, development, transport facilities and infrastructure? How can the capital of a landscape be explained?

Here, the joint search for terminologies that explore the phenomenon of landscape perception across cultures and societies proved to be both crucial and extremely challenging.[1] Accordingly, we recognised that a thematic cycle of semesters at the beginning of our research would prove to be too restrictive.

[1] See also www.charta-vierwaldstättersee.ch

Photo by BECK Jürgen

Thus, the basic thematic concepts were defined together, building up organically, in the knowledge of the work already completed before each upcoming semester. Lake Biwa and Lake Lucerne are the centrepiece of their respective country – not only geographically, but also politically and culturally, and, as national symbols, they have far-reaching appeal that has connected them deeply with people for centuries. Our central fields of research "Danger, beauty, community and eternity" proved to be as monumental as the questions that developed out of them. We found ourselves in an open project investigating the significance of water for the inland environment of two such different cultures, which on closer inspection could be so similar.

Soba in Itsutsu 五, Kyoto, 2023

It became apparent that our own methods of research, analysis and ultimately the conception of the architectural project as a possible answer to the outlined hypothesis had to be repeatedly questioned and scrutinised in the exchanges with our partners. Did we agree on how we wanted to express themes such as beauty or eternity architecturally with our students? Did we have to agree? It was precisely here that we reaped the profound moments of dialogue in which we understood that language is ultimately a physical expression of our environment.

The five-year collaboration on comparative research into water as a determining factor in the perception of our environment and our immediate actions in the midst of these landscapes ultimately turned out to be an interdisciplinary and transcultural project with political, social and not least religious dimensions. The ambitious and unusual length of this academic examination of the other and our own culture fostered learning about the deep roots of our societies in the lake landscapes of Lake Biwa and Lake Lucerne. One didactic approach of our studies was to show and explain our own environment in its complex depth to the "foreign" counterpart; the dialectical counterpart was revealed by listening and immersing oneself in the foreign.

Katsura Imperial Villa 桂離宮, Kyoto, 2018

This seems as simple as it is self-evident. But how does academic collaboration take place over a time difference of eight hours and a distance of 10,000 kilometres? We began in a similar way as with previous projects with other universities. The respective design studios of up to 14 students worked in parallel on the same task – in autumn on Lake Biwa and in spring in the context of Central Switzerland around Lake Lucerne. A ten-day seminar trip during the semester brought students and teaching teams together at the location that we studied. Introductory lectures by professors from the respective universities and other guests placed the topic of the semester in a cultural and socio-political context. Field trips and visits to important historical and contemporary architecture enabled an initial exploration of the depth and complexity of social expression. We got to know each other; we ate, drank and sang karaoke to-

Nishikigoi 錦鯉, Myoshin-ji 妙心寺, Kyoto, 2018

gether. The great distance only allowed the students one trip per semester. However, the lecturers from both studios came together again for the final critiques to discuss the students' projects and the insights gained from them.

The energy and intensity of our collaboration then changed completely and unexpectedly during the coronavirus pandemic. Instead of cancelling the five-year project, we seized the opportunity presented by the new communication technologies and intensified the exchange between students and lecturers. Physical boundaries seemed to be overcome for the time being. Lectures could be held weekly for all students. Joint workshops and intercontinental group work became part of the didactic concept. Project discussions as part of the interim and final critiques enabled all student work to be recognised and a shared knowledge base to be built up. The time difference meant that everyone was prepared to present and discuss well past midnight or to begin in the earliest hours of the morning. Our intercultural cooperation was unforeseen raised to a new level.

The findings and projects published in this book are of course not intended to be exhaustive. They are testimony to a committed and intensive intercultural and friendly exchange, which ultimately brings home to us the fragility of our relationships with the two lake landscapes and their timeless scale. In this sense, we see the present work as a contribution to living cultures on and by both bodies of water, which should bridge further centuries.

Weggis, Lake Lucerne, 2023

Atlas of Switzerland by Meyer, Weiss and Müller, 1796–1802 (detail)

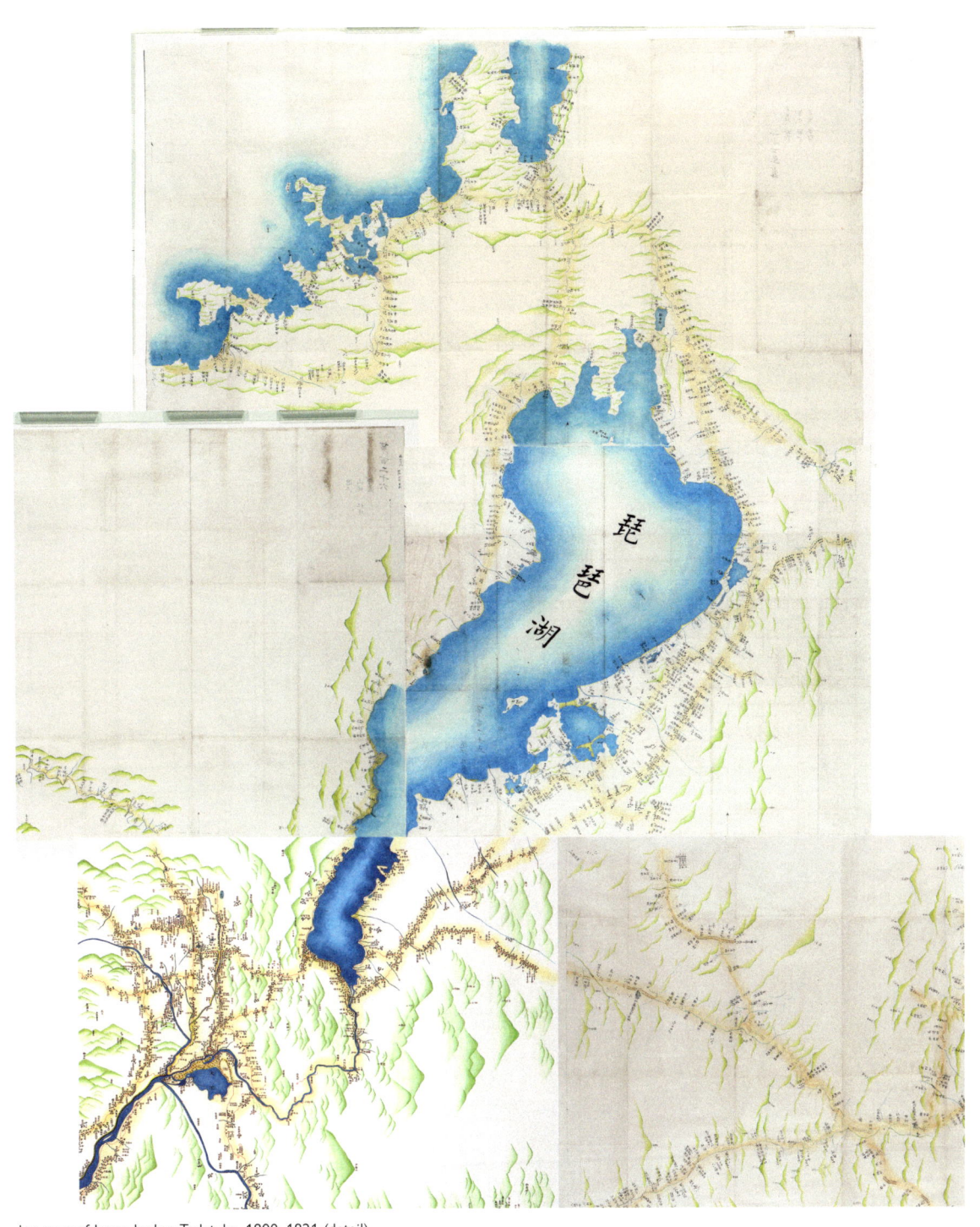

Ino map of Japan by Ino Tadataka, 1800–1821 (detail)

FOUR TOPICS –
EIGHT AMBITIONS
４つの視点−８つの展望

GEISSBÜHLER Dieter and SUN BUSCHOR Mulan

The title of this research project, "The Culture of Water", refers in a broad sense to the influence of water on architecture along the two fresh water lakes: Lake Lucerne (Vierwaldstättersee), the mythological heart of Switzerland and Lake Biwa, the largest fresh water reservoir in Japan. For every culture the relation to water determines very specific interpretations in architecture and in the organisation of settlements. This relation is on the one hand obvious and on the other hand hidden. For Switzerland fresh water is available in exuberance, while in Japan fresh water is scarce and thus more protected. This reality establishes a rather specific and different awareness in the two cultures. The narrative potential of water is immense and its role in architecture is distinctive. In the end and after productive discussions with the teams of instructors four topics were chosen: Danger, Beauty, Commons and Eternity. Together with the alternating location on both lakes and the distinct change of culture the outcome were eight ambitions that allow an understanding of similarities and differences. This made this bicultural and paedagogical experiment a rich experience for all participants and provides an insight for all readers of this publication.

Water & Danger	Lake Lucerne	Hazard Map
	Lake Biwa	Hazard Map
Water & Beauty	Lake Lucerne	Hidden Beauty
	Lake Biwa	Eight Views of Ōmi
Water & Commons	Lake Lucerne	Productivity
	Lake Biwa	Ritual
Water & Eternity	Lake Lucerne	Stone
	Lake Biwa	Re-Metabolism

Water and Danger: The challenge of bringing the force of water under control – the development of specific design strategies and scenarios to reflect on the impact of natural hazards on architecture for protection.

Water and Beauty: This topic is less about pure aesthetics than about a more broadly and openly defined concept of beauty that includes the perception of architecture as well as its different meanings in two cultural settings.

Water and Commons: Water is not a commodity, water is a common resource both in a productive as well as in a spiritual sense, in combination with ritual.

Water and Eternity: With an eye on the long history of both lakes and on a possible future, we rethink the concept of eternity and ask ourselves the question: "What is and what does eternity mean regarding nature and human beings?"

Photo by BECK Jürgen

HAZARD MAPS OF LAKE LUCERNE

GEISSBÜHLER Dieter
with KIMURA Hiroyuki

"Whatever is fitted in any sort to excite the ideas of pain and danger, that is to say, whatever is in any sort terrible, or is conversant about terrible objects, or operates in a manner analogous to terror, is a source of the sublime; that is, it is productive of the strongest emotion which the mind is capable of feeling …. When danger or pain press too nearly, they are incapable of giving any delight …. but …. with certain modifications, they may be, and they are, delightful, as we every day experience."

Edmund Burke, *A Philosophical Enquiry into the Origin of our Ideas of the Sublime and Beautiful*, 1757

WATER AND SWITZERLAND, LAKE REGION

Water in general is an extremely central aspect of Swiss culture, especially in the culture of the Alps. This is primarily caused by its direct, physical impact. It is about physical power, made apparent in the change of the earth's surface through the influence of water. In this sense, especially in the mountains, the threat of water has a high social and practical significance.

Interestingly, it was these threatening forces of nature that aroused fascination in art in the mid-19th century. It is probably no coincidence that John Ruskin used the depiction of the "sublime", as represented in William Turner's paintings of his travels along Lake Lucerne, to illustrate this remarkable change in perception of aesthetic values. In contrast to this aestheticisation of the dangerous, protection determines human existence in a very direct, almost pragmatic way. Protection from the dangers of nature has been understood as a collective task since early times and this common chore was a key factor in the union of the

Water & Danger	Lake Lucerne	Hazard Map
	Lake Biwa	Hazard Map
Water & Beauty	Lake Lucerne	Hidden Beauty
	Lake Biwa	Eight Views of Ōmi
Water & Commons	Lake Lucerne	Productivity
	Lake Biwa	Ritual
Water & Eternity	Lake Lucerne	Stone
	Lake Biwa	Re-Metabolism

mountain cantons around Lake Lucerne in the early Swiss Confederation. For the Alpine region, the main threats are sudden floods, rapidly melting snow and storms with rain or snow, as well as avalanches at higher altitudes. In recent years, however, the extended dry seasons and the loosening of the surface layers associated with the retreat of permafrost and the melting of glaciers have also contributed to the increasing complexity of natural hazards. The canton of Nidwalden and the Beckenried area in particular are an example of this, with a density of potential hazard areas that is exceptional, even for Switzerland.

DANGER AND HAZARD MAPS

In 18th-century Switzerland, disasters were regarded as a punishment of god, but a series of natural catastrophes in the mid-19th century led to modern engineering research and countermeasures. This major change in perception coincided with the completion of Switzerland's first modern survey topographic map, the Dufour map of 1845–1865. Switzerland thereafter took a leading position in this field of research.

Today, hazards are comprehensively mapped in Switzerland and zones with differentiated hazard potential are identified. The Swiss government focuses on the protection of buildings against natural hazards on four levels: 1. Planning measures – regulating the design of buildings so that their envelope and load-bearing structure contain a minimum amount of vulnerable areas; 2. Technical measures – for example automatic bulkhead, wind sensors for sunscreens, etc.; 3. Material choices – promoting the use of robust materials; 4. Organisational tasks – dictating rules of conducts such as closing windows when leaving the house, installation of temporary protection devices, etc.

Thus, the current strategy towards dealing with natural hazards is rather technical and the topic has not fully entered yet the realm of a broader architectural approach.

STUDENT RESEARCH: SHAPING HAZARD

Above all, the acceptance of transformation has to become the main purpose of the design process. The interventions of the students were located along a highway viaduct placed on "moving" land, that means in an area with increased potential of destruction through natural danger. The specific task was to respond to the situation by proposing an architectural approach. For the research, each student could choose a section of land within the area between Risleten and Buochs in the Canton of Nidwalden, from the steep land facing north into the lake. It is a long slope with a surface that is in constant flow, sliding slowly but steadily on top of a stable rockbase. Precautions taken against natural haz-

Hazard map of Beckenried

ards have a long tradition in this region and mainly consisted of controlling the flow of surface water. This area was chosen in order to find relevant answers to the problem of protection against natural hazards as an architectural (not a technical) task. Nidwalden has been selected according to data from maps of danger exposure and additional planning data issued by the Canton and the communities. Each student will develop his or her own strategy to facilitate living in that area in the coming years.

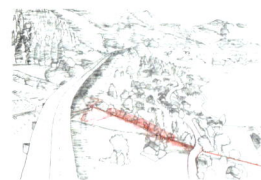

SAKAKI Kazusa: Trans-water, Beckenried

STUDENT PROJECT: RETOUCHING LANDSCAPE

The answers in the students' projects were extremely varied and involved the direct architectural articulation of functional aspects. In most cases, the reduction of the flow velocity in the rather steep terrain along the highway viaduct was achieved by widening the mostly canalised flood channels. The answers ranged from a purely creative staging of the water flow to a project for a covered market hall whose sculpturally modulated floor could absorb the water volumes in the event of flooding.

As these risky conditions are rare, occurring only three to five times a year for a few days, SAKAKI Kazusa proposed a disaster prevention space that could be used as a place to sell local products during normal times. Infrastructural components that temporarily store water and slow down the flow of water during a flood contribute to the community and townscape with architectural qualities.

The project by OTHMAN Afifah proposed an even more radical approach to containing the threatening flow velocity of large volumes of water. The inner area of a relatively densely populated settlement, from which traditionally any flooding should be kept away, was conceived as an actual dispersal area for any floods that occur. The resulting design measures, both for the buildings and the open space, were set out as guidelines within model rules of conduct. The result was a highly specific architectural and landscape design image of a settlement with a new identity-creating appearance.

WUST Max's project is spiritually influenced by an overarching view of danger as a metaphor. The idea of protection against the threat to our existence was taken up in a former quarry with a crematorium. In this special place, embedded in the confines of the pit hewn out of the rock, this capsule for spiritual concentration is carved out when people are bid farewell from earthly life.

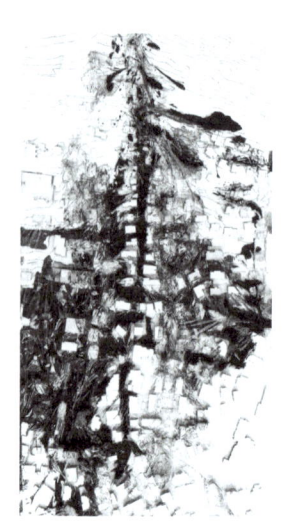

OTHMAN Afifah:
Testing the narrative, Buochs

Isle of the Dead: Basel version, Arnold Böcklin, 1880

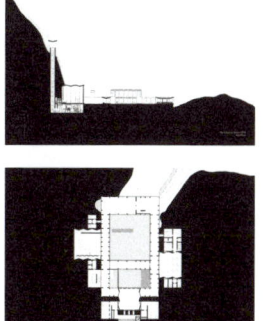

WUST Max: Crematory in the quarry, Beckenried

HAZARD MAPS OF LAKE BIWA

KIMURA Hiroyuki
with GEISSBÜHLER Dieter

柳に雪折れなし
Willow trees never break
under the weight of snow

JAPAN AND THREATS

There is a Japanese proverb that says: "Earthquake, Thunder, Fire and Father". The proverb consists simply of a list of four threat words and does not have a didactic sentence structure like most proverbial sayings. This peculiar proverb was rather easy to commit to memory because of its humorous wording and pleasant rhyme. Its first written appearance is in a collection of nursery rhymes from the mid-19th century. Beyond the topic of the threat to life itself, the proverb gives us an idea of the thought and wisdom of our ancestors who passed it on from generation to generation.

DANGER FOR LAKE BIWA

Focusing on the Lake Biwa area, there were of course earthquakes and fires, but the most immediate danger has been flooding. Lake Biwa has a basin area five times the size of the lake, with 460 rivers of all sizes flowing into it. In addition to flooding caused by rising lake waters, there was also the danger of these rivers overflowing. Most floods occurred during summer rains and typhoons, but on rare occasions there were also snowmelt floods in early spring. The largest was the Great Lake Biwa Flood of 1896, when the water level of Lake Biwa reached +3.67 metres and flooding lasted for 237 days.

Droughts, the opposite of floods, are also a danger at Lake Biwa. Today, it is said that 14.5 million people, including citizens of Kyoto, depend on the Lake Biwa water system as their source of water. In fact, the Lake Biwa system is responsible for the lives of more than 10 percent of Japan's entire population. For this reason, efforts have been made to make the most effective use of the water resources, so much so that it is said that between Lake Biwa and the mouth of Osaka Bay, the water is repeatedly used as tap water, as much as five times. In addition, more

Water & Danger	Lake Lucerne	Hazard Map
	Lake Biwa	Hazard Map
Water & Beauty	Lake Lucerne	Hidden Beauty
	Lake Biwa	Eight Views of Ōmi
Water & Commons	Lake Lucerne	Productivity
	Lake Biwa	Ritual
Water & Eternity	Lake Lucerne	Stone
	Lake Biwa	Re-Metabolism

than twice the amount used as tap water in private households is used for agricultural and industrial purposes, making it the basis of the local ecosystem. Therefore, the water flow in the Lake Biwa system should not be disrupted. In the last 30 years of recorded recent history, water supply has been restricted on three occasions: In 1994, when the record low of 1.23 metres was recorded, it lasted for 40 days. In contrast to floods, which are visible disasters that strike at certain times, droughts are silent and slow-approaching catastrophes. And once they occur, they are a very frightening threat that can be long-lasting.

DISASTER PREVENTIONS: THE PAST

As a countermeasure, the comprehensive development of Lake Biwa was undertaken and improved as a 25-year long project from 1972: 12 new dams and weirs were built, the lake's shores were strengthened and such measures were carried out using modern technology and large quantities of concrete. This stabilised the lake level and increased not only safety but also convenience. During the same period, on the other hand, lifestyles were drastically transformed and the industrial structure also experienced significant changes. As a result of these interactions, communities have become less and less connected, and people's direct engagement with Lake Biwa has also decreased drastically. As a consequence, the village landscape and the biological environment of Lake Biwa have changed dramatically.

Local communities' voluntary disaster management groups have been replaced by the government's top-down disaster management policy. This has ensured a certain level of safety on all fronts, but it has also led to a disconnection of the local community from the lives of its residents.

STUDENT RESEARCH: LIVING WITH HAZARD

The students conducted their research on the western shore of Lake Biwa, focusing on a narrow, steeply sloping area between the lake and the Hira Mountains. What was proposed there was an intervention more akin to a civil infrastructure or landscape than a stand-alone building. It probably contains naïve proposals with dimensionally different levels of load-bearing capacity from a civil engineering point of view.

By examining the hazard maps, the students realised the isolation brought about by hazards on livelihoods. Many of the students' suggestions were about living with hazards and not fighting them head-on, but yielding to them tactfully. It was as kung fu master Bruce Lee said, "Yielding will overcome anything superior to itself; its strength is boundless." The approach is reminiscent of the Japanese proverb of the willow that does not break under the snow.

STUDENT PROJECT: THE FUTURE

UEBAYASHI Yoshiya chose a site near Kitakomatsu Station in Ōtsu City, on the steep western shore of Lake Biwa. A public open space was planned beside a creek that runs right beside the station to provide a place for cyclists, high school students on their way to school and other passers-by in the vicinity. At the same time, it was to have the function of mitigating flood damage when the creek rises. The narrow width of the creek causes it to rapidly rise and flood in the event of heavy rainfall. However, a strategy was developed that was opposite to the conventional idea of fortifying the creek with a revetment. When the water level rises, the creek is dispersed into a number of squares as multiple streams with low water velocities, which are then drained downstream into the ditches of the housing estate road. Rather than forcefully isolating the risk of flooding from the residential areas, an approach was proposed in which the weakened risk would be present alongside everyday living space.

UEBAYASHI Yoshiya framed these concepts with reference to local heritage, such as the traditional stone masons in the area known as "ano-shu" and the "Hyakken-tsutsumi", an embankment built of giant stones.

NOMURA Kano researched and designed the Oya River in Ōtsu City as her site.

The Oya River is fed by the Hira Mountains, a scenic area known for Hira no Kureyuki, one of the Eight Views of Ōmi. The river is a subterranean river, which is common in the region, and the surface water only flows in times of heavy rainfall. Concrete-reinforced riverbanks, as in many cases, divide the river space from the surrounding environment. The result is a lost space, where no one can come close except in the sandy river delta area. NOMURA Kano's proposal is to install a 500-metre promenade alongside the river from the bridge near the village to the river delta. However, this is not a "safe at all times" infrastructure, but one that will be overflowed when the water level rises. An observation platform is also proposed at the foot of the bridge, where visitors can check the flooding conditions. This intervention not only provides the neighbourhood with a shortcut to the delta beach, but also makes them more familiar with the conditions of the river and its dangers.

UEBAYASHI Yoshiya: Stone cave, Ōtsu

MARTINEZ Manuel worked on a site on Mt Karausu in Ōtsu City. There is a burial mound there, which is said to be the tomb of Ono no Imoko (a 7th-century diplomat), and the Ono Shrine, which is dedicated to him. Today, the area is surrounded by large-scale housing developments of recent years. The existence of this heritage site seems to have become irrelevant to the nearby residents, who appear to have little sense of community. In fact, the Konpira Shrine further up the site has been abandoned recently. Despite an increase in the num-

NOMURA Kano: Disappeared park, Oya River, Ōtsu

ber of nearby residents, its building has fallen into decay in the absence of any caretaker.

MARTINEZ Manuel's project was to safely reinforce the slope of Mt Karausu first, which had been exposed as a result of housing development works, to prevent landslides. At the same time, the rational design of the reinforcement allowed for the construction of a promenade and a meeting place (which could also serve as an emergency shelter). In this way, the historical heritage hillside was transformed from a neglected and dangerous place into a safe space for everyone to gather, both in normal conditions and in times of disaster.

MARTINEZ Manuel:
Reinforcement of Mt Karausu

HIDDEN BEAUTY

MOLO Ludovica
WETTSTEIN Felix

"We are subject to *venustas,* not *firmitas;* it is
beauty that enchants us, that makes us curious
about life and ourselves, that awakens and stimu-
lates us."

Jacques Herzog

LAKE LUCERNE – AN ABSOLUTE BEAUTY?

Lake Lucerne and its landscape are undoubtedly perceived as beautiful. The
horizontal surface of the lake contrasts with the mostly steep slopes and the
striking mountains on the horizon. Unspoiled natural landscapes, intact settlement structures and impressing infrastructure are part of an overall picture that
is read as the "Swiss myth". On closer inspection, however, even this supposedly
perfect landscape shows cracks and fissures. The pressure exerted by modern
society leads to conflicts of interest that leave their mark on land use, from industrial areas to urban sprawl.

We were searching for the "hidden beauty" in these places. The beauty of a
site is not always visible and has to be discovered first. Is there a hidden beauty
under the cloak of banality? How can this beauty be discovered and kissed
awake?

We looked at these problematic and "unsightly" locations, the places that
have potential for improvement in terms of urban development and architecture. The places are located at the ends, at the tips of Lake Lucerne, where the
urban areas are located due to the topographical conditions. They are characterised by industrial areas, infrastructure buildings and mostly poor architecture.
Urban development is not present – as is often the case on the periphery, at
the difficult transitions between city and countryside.

Water & Danger	Lake Lucerne	Hazard Map
	Lake Biwa	Hazard Map
Water & Beauty	Lake Lucerne	Hidden Beauty
	Lake Biwa	Eight Views of Ōmi
Water & Commons	Lake Lucerne	Productivity
	Lake Biwa	Ritual
Water & Eternity	Lake Lucerne	Stone
	Lake Biwa	Re-Metabolism

JANA MULLE _ THE SPACE IN BETWEEN

Brunnen is known for its prominent location at the transition from Lake Uri to Lake Gersau. From the prestigious lakeside promenade, the view sweeps eastwards to the Bürgenstock and southwards to the Gotthard massif. Brunnen owes its importance as a tourist resort on Lake Lucerne to this scenic beauty. Less attractive is the rear of the village, where the river, railroad, highway and roads are squeezed into a confined space. MULLE Jana has taken on this forgotten and conflict-ridden location. She complements the existing buildings with light, ephemeral structures and uses them to enliven the public space. In doing so, she discovers the hidden beauty of the existing buildings, the diversity, the space in between, and thus gives a face and an independent public life to a place that has maintained a shadowy existence to this day. The attention and careful upgrading give the public space back its dignity, life and thus its specific beauty.

THE TRANSCENDENTALISTS' TRUTH, GOODNESS AND BEAUTY

Lake Lucerne corresponds to the Western concept of beauty, which goes back to Greek philosophy. The allure of beauty captivated the ancient Greeks to an unparalleled extent, surpassing prior and subsequent societies. Arguably, the most impactful exploration of beauty during this era stems from Plato's Socratic dialogues. Within these dialogues, Plato defines beauty as one of the ultimate values, alongside truth and justice. He posits that if something possesses beauty, it inherently holds moral goodness. According to Plato, the intertwining of

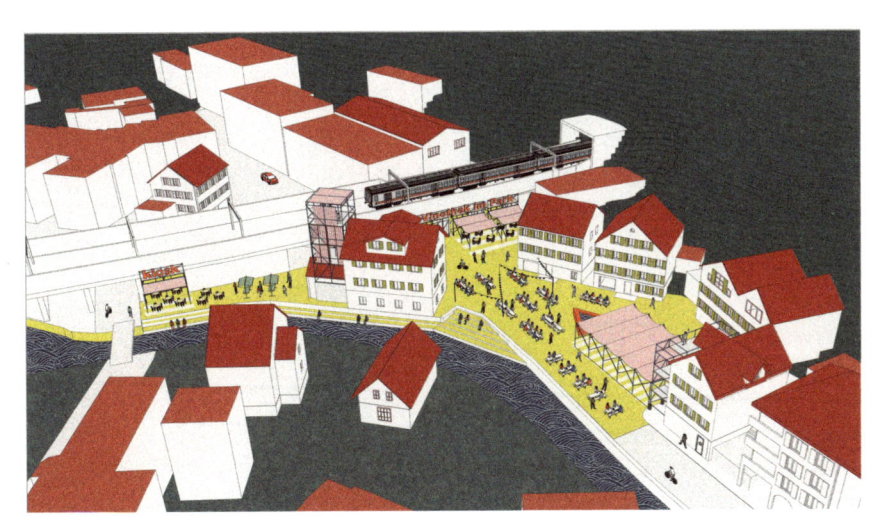

MULLE Jana: The space in between, Brunnen

beauty and goodness is reciprocal – whatever is good is beautiful, and whatever is beautiful is also good. Additionally, Plato extends his perspective by equating beauty with truth and truth with beauty.

Throughout the centuries, renowned philosophers have labeled truth, goodness and beauty as transcendentals – cosmic values that exist beyond the confines of the time-space-matter world. The term "transcendental" denotes a universal reality that surpasses our everyday sensory experiences, characterised as non-physical, immaterial, conceptual or even spiritual. In the realm of philosophy, the transcendental seeks to elucidate the nature of reality or being, portraying these values as timeless universals and inherent attributes of existence.

Therefore, Western beauty ideals often revolve around the pursuit of perfection, influenced by classical Greek notions of ideal forms. The emphasis is on flawless symmetry and proportion. At the same time the Western concept often values beauty that appears timeless and unchanging.

Vitruvius, the most important architect and architectural theorist of Roman antiquity also described *venustas,* i.e., beauty, as the most important requirement of architecture alongside *firmitas* and *utilitas,* strength and usability. Until the early 20th century, the five orders of columns were regarded as the essential structural system in architectural education. This knowledge formed the basis for harmonious proportions and the pursuit of order. Beauty was defined with precise rules, with numbers and measures and thus with mathematics. With modernism, *utilitas* gained the upper hand over *venustas* and "form follows function" became the new dictum. Beauty took a back seat and was limited to the result of a functional approach. Since then, we have struggled with the concept of beauty questioning the idea of a universal standard, embracing diversity and often celebrating the unconventional.

The term has been largely banished from teaching and architectural discourse. More recently, however, there has been a noticeable change in thinking. We once again dare to think about beauty without being labeled as old-fashioned. This is less about pure aesthetics and more about an expanded and more openly defined concept of beauty that encompasses perception as well as the meaning and sustainability of architecture.

AL JAWHARAH AL ZAMIL _ A BOWL IN THE WATER
Küssnacht lies at the tip of the north-eastern arm of Lake Lucerne. The town is primarily known for the Rigi, the Queen of the Mountains, which lies to the south. The horizontal surface of the lake forms the perfect counterpoint to the majestic topography of the mountains. AL JAWHARAH al Zamil has carefully studied the horizontality of the water surface. Through precise research, she discovered that

the lake's water level is regulated, but not constant. The difference in height between the lowest levels in winter and the highest levels in early summer due to meltwater is around 50 centimetres. A circular, funnel-shaped bowl with a radius of 100 metres lies in the water. The water enters the bowl via an opening at the lowest point and spreads out depending on the water level, whereby the outer ring always remains accessible. The pool becomes a magical attraction, inviting visitors to linger and bathe. Beyond this, however, it tells the story of the lake mirror and the perfection of geometry. The result is poetry and pure beauty.

WABI-SABI

Interestingly, the Japanese culture seems to have a more relaxed approach to beauty than the Western world, despite the fact that aesthetics is celebrated in all areas of life, from the preparation of food to the design of gardens and architecture.

The Japanese aesthetic philosophy Wabi-Sabi embraces the beauty of imperfection, transience and simplicity. Originally, the term "wabi" conveyed a sense of misery, loneliness and being lost. Over time, this evolved into an appreciation for the joy found in the austerity of solitude and silence. The true depth of this concept emerged when paired with "sabi" – the quality of being old, showing patina and possessing maturity. This unique combination forms an untranslatable conceptual unit that has become the standard in Japanese art appreciation.

In this philosophy, the highest form of beauty is not overt but veiled, not the direct brilliance of the sun but the refracted light of the moon. Objects like the mossy rock, grassy thatched roof, gnarled pine tree and slightly rusty tea kettle are emblematic of this ideal beauty. They serve as symbols of the majesty concealed within the seemingly inconspicuous, representing an austere simplicity that reveals the charms of beauty to those with a nuanced understanding. Beyond visual aesthetics, Wabi-Sabi influences a broader approach to life, emphasising imperfection, maturity and an acknowledgement of the transient nature of existence. Wabi-Sabi sees imperfections as integral to the essence of beauty. A cracked tea bowl or a weathered piece of pottery is not discarded but cherished for the uniqueness and history it carries.

Simplicity and modesty lie at the heart of Japanese aesthetics. It esteems the unadorned and the understated, embracing minimalism in both design and lifestyle. At the centre lies a profound connection to nature. Drawing inspiration from the irregularities inherent in rocks, plants and landscapes, this aesthetic philosophy encourages the integration of nature into daily life. Practices such as incorporating bonsai trees or arranging simple floral displays serve to bring the serene beauty of the outdoors indoors.

AL ZAMIL Al Jawharah:
A bowl in the water, Küssnacht

It nourishes everything that is authentic, as it recognises three simple truths: nothing remains, nothing is complete and nothing is perfect.

Richard R. Powell

OKINO JUN _ MUSIC IN THE MIRROR

The city, the lake, the mountains – and the music. Lucerne is praised as a city of music. Jean Nouvel's KKL is already an architectural jewel in the most prominent location. Further south, on a headland, the composer Richard Wagner lived in the Tribschen country house in the middle of the 19th century. Today, the house with its large park is open to the public as the Richard Wagner Museum. OKINO Jun has added a concert hall to the museum. More than a hall, it is a space in the park. The rectangular room is defined by 6-metre-high, mirrored steles. These are aligned to create optimal acoustic conditions. As in René Magritte's famous painting The Blank Signature, different levels, foreground, and background interweave to create a new, mysterious world. The mirror, as a symbol of the immaterial, thus reflects not only the nature of the park, but also the sound of the music. Image and sound, appearance and truth combine to create a uniquely beautiful space.

"Beauty is not a marginal luxury that our society can or cannot afford; it is a vital dimension and a prerequisite for culture."

Vittorio Magnago Lampugnani

OKINO Jun:
Soundscape, Lucerne

BEAUTY FOUND THROUGH "EIGHT VIEWS OF ŌMI"

KINOSHITA Masahiro

WHERE IS BEAUTY?

We asked a bold question and searched for a clue in the "Eight Views of Ōmi", a series of eight famous vistas around Lake Biwa that were produced as ukiyo-e prints.

The "Eight Views of Ōmi", commemorating specific landmarks in the southern part of Lake Biwa, were first described in waka poems in the early 17th century and were later painted as ukiyo-e in the latter half of the 17th century. They show the scenery of the time and the people passing through this landscape. To what extent are the scenes painted realistically, thus reflecting contemporary conditions? Even though the role of Ukiyo-e is to convey famous places widely, there is no doubt that the characteristics of the painted objects are exaggerated and that the viewpoints chosen to depict each place would in reality be too difficult to reach. In other words, the Eight Views of Ōmi are not objective renderings of actual landscapes, but rather reconstructions. Through the mediation of the poem, the landscape is transformed into a scene that contains not only visual information, but also auditory and tactile phenomena, as well as the flow of time. The eight views of Ōmi capture a beautiful moment, the superimposition of a specific season, weather, scenery and human emotions and activities.

Thus, beauty arises in the moment.

IS THERE BEAUTY IN OUR TIME?

The Eight Views of Ōmi were painted to capture beautiful moments. Today, the scenery around Lake Biwa is not the same. Over the course of time, the shores of the lake have been reclaimed for agriculture and residential areas and developed to prevent flood damage. The scenery once created by water, nature and human activity has been lost, and it is now difficult to recover it. Is it still possible to find beauty in this altered landscape? Is it possible to create beauty anew? How could we draw the eight views of Ōmi in the present time? This was the challenge of this joint studio.

Water & Danger	Lake Lucerne	Hazard Map
	Lake Biwa	Hazard Map
Water & Beauty	Lake Lucerne	Hidden Beauty
	Lake Biwa	Eight Views of Ōmi
Water & Commons	Lake Lucerne	Productivity
	Lake Biwa	Ritual
Water & Eternity	Lake Lucerne	Stone
	Lake Biwa	Re-Metabolism

The first step was to undertake research on the eight landscapes that had been painted in the past and on the changes in those locations over time and, while keeping a sober eye on the current situation, try to find new moments of beauty in those sceneries. By resorting to some architectural intervention, I thought it would be possible to create a moment of beauty when human activity and the changes created by nature coincide.

The students, who were divided into groups, with each group assigned to one of those eight famous places, explored their own ways to create eight beautiful contemporary landscapes.

Utagawa Hiroshige: Clear Breeze at Awazu, 粟津晴嵐

FLOATING, WAVERING

Work 1 "KAPPA" by BAER Rebecca

Travel by boat on Lake Biwa has been replaced by land routes and therefore the number of boats has decreased considerably. However, the abundance of water, the expression of its surface, and the rhythm of its fluctuations have not changed, and have an eternal quality. This design proposes a pavilion floating on the lake that incorporates the fluctuations of the water level into its architecture. The pavilion will travel around Lake Biwa, at times becoming a theatre, that can also be used for showing movies, and at other times a restaurant. Rebecca Baer likened the floating pavilion to the kappa, an imaginary creature from ancient Japan. She created a beautiful moment in which the kappa appears and disappears.

BAER Rebecca: Kappa – A floating pavilion on Lake Biwa

WATER CIRCULATING, PEOPLE CIRCULATING

Work 2 "Water Bridge of Yabase" by KOJIMA Hiroki

Water flows into Lake Biwa from the surrounding mountains. At the same time, water used for agriculture and daily life is also released into the lake. The port of Yabase used to be a landing place for boats connecting this side of the lake to the other, but now the boats have disappeared, and only the shape of the lakeshore remains as a reminder. Furthermore, an artificial island built by landfill in front of the former harbour blocks even the view to the other side of the lake.

A sewage purification facility has been built on the artificial island. The island, which incorporates a facility that is by no means beautiful, was built to cleanse waste water and return clean water to Lake Biwa, clearly an improvement over the days when sewage flowed directly into the lake and contaminated its water. This proposal visualises the relationship between people's lives and water by giving a tangible form to the beautiful act of purification.

The forms created by water change from moment to moment: the water flowing down, the light piercing the water and the sound of water. A new picture was painted to capture the beautiful compositions created by these elements.

Utagawa Hiroshige: Returning Sails at Yabase 矢橋歸帆

KOJIMA Hiroki: Water bridge of Yabase

BRIDGE OVERLAY
Work 3 "Seta Bridge" by WEIBEL Werner

Out of Lake Biwa, where water flows in from the surrounding mountains, the Seta River, which is the only river flowing out of the lake, changes its name and becomes the Uji River in Kyoto and the Yodo River in Osaka. It thus also delivers water to Kyoto and Osaka. The Karahashi Bridge over the Seta River was once a strategic point in the historic road network and the scene of many battles but its role has changed over time. Today, the bridge is mainly used for automobiles and only the shape of the bridge remains as it was in the past.

Bridges not only serve as a connection between one place and another, but they are also symbolic entities that link two elements. Moreover, they are places where the river flowing under the bridge and people crossing the bridge intersect. To reconstruct the lost potential of bridges with these multiple meanings, a proposal was made to build a new bridge over the existing one, which would not only functionally separate cars and pedestrians, but would also form a site of its own and give a sense of excitement to those crossing. A new bridge creates a new landscape.

SCENERY CREATED BY PEOPLE AND PINE TREES
Work 4 "Future Karasaki Pine Tree" by KANAZAWA Misato

Pine forests planted as windbreaks to protect against the strong winds from the lake once made up the scenery of the shore of Lake Biwa. Although they still exist, the extent of these windbreaks has been drastically reduced, as today's stronger buildings no longer require them. The Karasaki pine tree at Karasaki Shrine is a pine tree that was a functional windbreak, but was revered as a symbolic and sacred tree. This ritual has been passed down from generation to generation, and the pine trees are still preserved and nurtured. However, as the number of people who take care of the pine trees has decreased and the continuation of this task is in serious jeopardy, this proposal lets the act of tending to the pine trees create a new landscape. The scene that ensues from the collaboration of people and pine trees can be understood as one of the "Eight Views of Ōmi" of today.

COLLABORATION WITH NATURE
The discovery of beauty through the "Eight Views of Ōmi" was not about the unchanging beauty that can be permanently maintained by architecture alone, but about finding the beauty of the moment in a scene that is constantly changing. It is a beauty that can only come about through the relationship between architecture, nature and human behaviour. What kind of beautiful moments arise in the future will depend on how a harmonious relationship with nature can evolve.

Utagawa Hiroshige: Evening Glow at Seta 瀬田夕照

WEIBEL Werner: A new bridge in Seta

Utagawa Hiroshige: Evening Rain at Karasaki 唐崎夜雨

KANAZAWA Misato: Future Karasaki pine tree

WATER AND COMMONS

DEON Luca, SEIFERT Annika
with KIMURA Hiroyuki

TWO LAKES

Lake Lucerne and Lake Biwa emerge as emblematic embodiments of cultural significance within their respective societal contexts. Both lakes transcend mere geographical features; they serve as symbols of cultural heritage, ecological balance and collective identity, inviting exploration of their roles within the broader context of the understanding of the commons.

In Switzerland, Lake Lucerne and its surroundings reflect a Swiss approach to water governance, which is deeply rooted in the principles of direct democracy and decentralised decision-making, ensuring that the management of water resources remains transparent, inclusive and accountable to the public. The lake is a central source of value of supra-regional importance – as a freshwater reservoir and means of transportation, through hydro-power and lake thermal energy, but also for the extraction of raw materials from and with the lake.

In Japan, Lake Biwa holds a sacred place in the memory of the Japanese people, symbolising the interconnectedness of humanity and nature. The approach and usage of water around the lake is characterised by a coexistence of traditional knowledge and modern management, just as the environment around the lake is a patchwork of privately owned natural inner-lakes and state-owned artificial coastlines.

In both Switzerland and Japan, the cultural and political dimensions of water governance intersect with broader debates about sustainability, equity and social justice. As architects and landscape planners, we are tasked with navigating these complexities, striving to create environments that honour the intrinsic value of water as a common resource while fostering resilience and adaptation in the face of global change. In doing so, it is worthwhile exploring the two different cultural understandings of the commons.

THE ECONOMICS OF SURVIVAL: COMMUNAL MANAGEMENT IN SWITZERLAND

Switzerland, stereotypically renowned for its picturesque landscapes and robust economy, has a long-standing tradition of embracing commons as an economic

Water & Danger	Lake Lucerne	Hazard Map
	Lake Biwa	Hazard Map
Water & Beauty	Lake Lucerne	Hidden Beauty
	Lake Biwa	Eight Views of Ōmi
Water & Commons	Lake Lucerne	Productivity
	Lake Biwa	Ritual
Water & Eternity	Lake Lucerne	Stone
	Lake Biwa	Re-Metabolism

strategy for collective survival. The history of commons in Switzerland trace back centuries, rooted in the communal management of resources by local communities. Historically, Swiss villages relied on collective management of resources such as alpine pastures, forests, waterways and village commons. These communal practices were governed by locally devised rules and norms, fostering cooperation, reciprocity and social cohesion within the community.

One significant tradition of commons in Switzerland is the management of alpine pastures, known as *Alpwirtschaft*. Alpine farming communities would collectively graze their livestock on shared mountain pastures during the summer months, employing traditional transhumance practices. Through cooperative efforts, villagers would regulate grazing rights, maintain infrastructure and allocate resources fairly among participants, ensuring the sustainable use of the alpine environment and fostering economic resilience. Until today, many Swiss municipalities, including Lucerne, still have a large area, the so-called *Allmend* (German for *Commons*), i.e. often an open green space, designated for public use, which dates back to the time when a shared common ground was the most sensible solution for grazing and haymaking down in the valley close to a settlement. Over time, use of these spaces has shifted from agricultural needs to military functions, trade and fun fairs, public sports grounds or natural reserves within the city boundaries.

Suone in Baltschiedertal, Canton of Valais, photo by Roland Zumbuehl, 2003

Another vital tradition of commons in Switzerland is found in the management of cultivated forests. In her seminal work *Governing the Commons,* the Swedish economist Elinor Ostrom cites the *Oberallmeindkorporation* in the canton of Schwyz, bordering Lake Lucerne, among the most ancient surviving cooperative enterprises, dating back almost a thousand years.[1] Historically, rural communities here relied on collective forest management practices to sustainably harvest timber, gather firewood and (unintentionally) preserve biodiversity. By implementing regulations and agreements, villagers ensured responsible forest use while supporting local livelihoods and maintaining ecological balance. Today, the corporation oversees 24,000 hectares of land, providing timber, stone, renewable energy and, of course, water.

In all these examples, management of the commons is simultaneously a question of water management. The tougher the natural conditions of the alpine surroundings, the more complex this management becomes. In Southern Switzerland, in the mountainous canton of Valais, the famous example of the *bisses* (German: *Suonen*) can be found – the historic irrigation channels, which transport precious water down from mountain streams to fields, vineyards and fruit orchards. The construction of these systems in dangerous topography and under precarious circumstances was necessary for economic success, some-

[1] Elinor Ostrom: *Governing the Commons. The Evolution of Institutions for Collective Action,* Cambridge 1990

times even for survival, but demanded a collective investment, sometimes paid for by the loss of individual lives.

In contemporary Switzerland, the traditions of commons continue to be reflected as economic strategies. Cooperative enterprises, such as Migros and Coop, exemplify this tradition by embodying principles of collective ownership, democratic governance and social responsibility. These retail cooperatives operate based on a cooperative system, with members collectively owning and managing enterprises, promoting economic democracy, social equity and environmental sustainability.

As a more spatially relevant practice, the formation of housing cooperatives represents another manifestation of a commons-based economic approach that encourage collective resilience against capitalist realities. Housing cooperatives provide affordable, collectively owned housing for members, governed democratically by residents. Through cooperative ownership and decision-making, housing cooperatives foster social inclusion, community engagement and sustainable development, ensuring access to housing for all and contributing to collective survival, including the more vulnerable, in urban areas. More often than not, these cooperatives look beyond the need for mere residential functions and explore mixed-use, co-working and other shared spaces, providing fertile ground for architectural and typological innovation.[2]

THE IRRATIONALITY OF SURVIVAL: IMMATERIAL COMMONS IN JAPAN

Japan enjoys extraordinary richness in natural resources, surrounded by diverse natural environments such as oceans, freshwater and forests, with a variety of so-called "72 seasons" ranging from a hot, rainy summer time to dry, freezing winters. While Western countries went through the Industrial Revolution and the subsequent social changes during the 18th and 19th centuries, Japan remained unchanged under the policy of isolation (1639–1854). When the Swiss Federal Institute of Technology was established and modern science was about to change the perception of the world, Japan was still a country of samurai with swords and people in kimonos, preserving its medieval-like society, traditions and indigenous way of life. The Edo period of isolation, also known as *Pax Tokugawa,* brought indeed two peaceful centuries without any wars, and was an exceptionally fruitful period in many aspects, especially in the field of cultural development.

After the opening of Japan to the outside world in 1854, rapid Westernisation (*Bunmei-kaika,* or civilisation and enlightenment) proceeded. While the ethnographic studies and preservation movements were dismantled by Westernisation, indigenous thinking and behaviour persisted in people's lives, sometimes on a subconscious level and below the Western surface.

Panorama of the Rütli meadow, photo by Piotr Metelski, SGG

[2] Angelika Juppien / Franziska Winterberger / Richard Zemp: *Innovative Wohnformen. Kontext, Typologien und Konsequenzen.* CCTP, Lucerne University of Applied Sciences (HSLU) 2019

The small fisherman's village of Sugaura, at the northern end of Lake Biwa, is a rather special example. Until 1996, there was no road and the village could only be reached by boat. The community is renowned for their specific mediaeval system of shared self-governance. In other areas on Lake Biwa, various commons-based practices, such as communal use of spring water (*Kabata* in Harie), can still be widely observed.

Summer festivals of the villages around the City of Ōmi-Hachiman also represent an example of commons around the Lake Biwa. Their focus are collaborative activities without any economical nor practical gain. In this regard, they are different from typical instances of commons where the distribution of material benefits is the main objective. While many of the seemingly unproductive activities such as rituals and festivals have disappeared in the course of modernisation, rationalism and individualism, some of these unproductive collaborative activities, or common rituals, have survived until the present day.

History has shown that modern foreign influences were perceived as frightening at the time but did not inflict substantial damage on the culture.

TRAGEDY OF THE COMMONS

In 1833, the British economist William Forster Lloyd with his essay "The Tragedy of the Commons", laid the foundations for a social science theory formulated 120 years later, according to which people have a tendency to over-use natural resources for their individual benefit without considering the welfare of a group or society as a whole. If a number of individuals only consider their own welfare in this way, it leads to negative outcomes for all, as the common resource is depleted.[3]

In plain view of this (proven) theory, the idea of the commons as an economic model, which proposes a community-based, more sustainable alternative to capitalist resource exploitation, has re-gained popularity in recent years. Therefore, the two semesters dealing with the topics of Water and Commons were dedicated to researching site-appropriate and context-specific ways of managing commons, as well as rules, rights and responsibilities for the management of a common good and how they are divided amongst a defined user community.

REVIVE THE COLLECTIVE!

Against the backdrop of observations on differences in the understanding of the commons in Switzerland and Japan, the students' discussion focused on different aspects of the location they were dealing with: for instance, the Lake Lucerne research prioritised the question of productivity. In Ostrom's theory, the suc-

[3] W. F. Lloyd: *Two Lectures on the Checks to Population,* Oxford 1833; Garrett Hardin: "The Tragedy of the Commons". In: *Science.* Vol. 162, Issue 3859, 1968, p. 1243–1248.

cess of the commons is based on clearly defined boundaries between legitimate users and non-authorised use. Through in-depth research of their chosen location, students each developed a differentiated idea of user groups and usage scenarios in which production should take place according to the principles of the commons. In addition to material goods, the object of production could then also be public space, or access to culture, education and other non-material values. Unsurprisingly, the projects at Lake Biwa were more concerned with the interaction of the communities amongst themselves and with nature than with a concrete idea of productivity.

Nevertheless, the exploration of the cultural differences in Swiss and Japanese commons traditions led to an enrichment of the respective concept of the collective in both contexts: in the projects at Lake Lucerne, a re-interpretation of traditional Swiss commons was achieved, more sensitised towards intangible aspects of community production, i.e. in the Japanese way, while the student projects around Lake Biwa involved a more material manifestation of common resources and their value, thus guided by the Swiss perception.

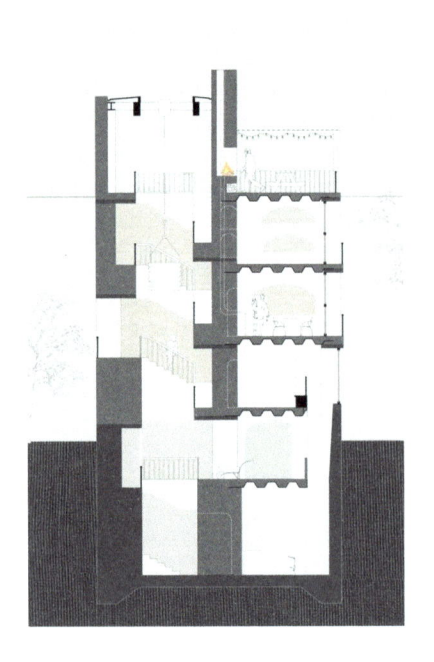

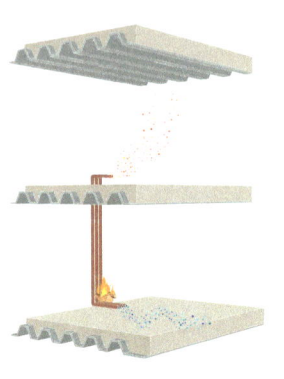

PURKIS Róisín: The Roost, a rammed-earth tower in Vitznau, which offers boating infrastructure for residents from around the lake. The thermo-spatial sequence from cool/wet towards warm-dry accommodates storage, repair, kitchen and simple lodging.

BAER Rebecca. Kulturbruch. An adaptable playground for community and culture in a deserted quarry. The interplay of permanent and temporary structures allows for a variety of programmatic scenarios.

MAKING OF RITUALS IN JAPAN HARE/KE AND SHITSURAI

KIMURA Hiroyuki

Religious views in Japan are the opposite of monotheistic, dogmatic beliefs and have a more regional and indigenous flavour. Throughout history, Shinto teachings and Buddhist concepts have been intricately intertwined with agrarian social practices and are inseparable.

The time and space of rituals has been recognised in Japan as the time and space of *Hare* (extraordinary) in contrast to *Ke* (ordinary). The time and space of *Hare* also includes many non-religious, agrarian and/or animistic customs and events. Over time, it has incorporated foreign influences, most significantly from China and Korea. Practised in various festivals and ritual events in daily life, it gained a very unique character especially in relation with the space. The space of *Hare* and the space of *Ke* can happen at the same place, just shifted on the time axis. More specifically, by applying the necessary *Shitsurai* (arrangements) on certain occasions, the space of *Ke* (ordinary, such as a living room) becomes the space of *Hare* (extraordinary, such as a festive place). Furthermore, a private realm can also be transformed into a public sphere through the *Shitsurai*. During the *Hare* time, not only the meaning of place, but also people's clothing, diet, behaviour and even language would be altered, creating a completely different universe for that moment.

In contemporary life, many rituals and events have diminished in response to modernisation, to changes of community and to changes of lifestyles. At the same time, they continue to exist, some in their original style, while others have been adapted. Some events have even gained more popularity through commercialisation. Additionally, new events have been initiated or imported. Despite various transformations and variations, notions of *Hare* and *Ke* can still be widely observed. This particular perception of time-space is the underlying foundation for the Japanese to shape and colour their lives, even today.

LAKE BIWA: WETLANDS, REEDS AND CYCLES

The Chronicles of Japan (8th century), one of the oldest surviving Japanese history books, describes Japan as "a country where reeds grow plentifully and grain

	Lake Lucerne	Hazard Map
Water & Danger	Lake Biwa	Hazard Map
Water & Beauty	Lake Lucerne	Hidden Beauty
	Lake Biwa	Eight Views of Ōmi
Water & Commons	Lake Lucerne	Productivity
	Lake Biwa	Ritual
Water & Eternity	Lake Lucerne	Stone
	Lake Biwa	Re-Metabolism

grows in abundance for ten thousand years". In addition to rice and wheat fields, Japan's archetypal landscape has been characterised by tall reeds growing thickly in wetlands. Indeed, reeds have played an essential part of everyday life in Japan, used for building materials, land improvement, fertilisers, food and fishing, and also for festivals and other events.

However, during the period of rapid economic growth in the second half of the 20th century, the demand for reeds declined rapidly due to the modernisation of lifestyle and culture. Correspondingly, reed beds have disappeared through the modernisation of lake shores. Today, the area around Lake Biwa's subsidiary (inner) lake is known as one of the few relict reed fields in Japan.

It is with this background that traditional culture and festivals using reeds are maintained at the area nearby the subsidiary lakes of Lake Biwa. (A similar example from Switzerland would be the straw burning festivals which can be observed also in the lakeside regions.)

Reed is a low-labour crop, requiring little help except for harvesting. The reeds are harvested communally in December, after the leaves fall off. In March, the bald field would be burned for better growth, and the heavy smoke is recognised as a feature of the season. Reed is not just about the summer festival, but has its roots in the community throughout the year.

Today, reeds are maintained and managed by communities in a conventional manner and as a common task. For a long time, they were far from sustainable in terms of continuity, as their growth was enabled only through the good will of individuals, namely private landowners, who sympathise with the conservation of reeds. Whenever there was a change in ownership, for instance through inheritance under private law, the production was at risk. With regard to forests, communal bodies similar to the Swiss *Korporation* were formed also in Japan, but this did not happen with regard to reeds. Finally, in 1993, Shiga prefectural government issued an ordinance to protect the reed fields and to eventually take over the land ownership. In the same year, it was declared a protected area under the Ramsar Convention. In this way, attention has been drawn to the wider environmental roles of the reeds which they have originally played. They are an essential part of the biological cycle as well as of the material and immaterial cycle: reeds do not only purify water (presenting a material, practical value), but also provide a habitat for plants, animals and insects on the water's edge (connected to an immaterial, social value).

EXTENDING SPECIFICITIES: PROPOSALS

In the semester on the theme of Rituals, students undertook a range of reflections and projects in a wide area of Lake Biwa.

Chikubushima is a small uninhabited island, where the entire island is regarded as a sacred site. Students proposed facilities such as a harbour as a threshold and a water treatment plant as a source of water for visitors, in order to enhance the pilgrimage place in a more sustainable way.

Okishima is an inhabited island in a freshwater lake, even today only accessible by boat. Proposals included a recycling centre, a hospice and a cemetery in the village, reflecting the specificity of the island community's material and spiritual structure.

Shitomido: square-lattice shutters or doors found on older-style Japanese buildings.

Nishinoko is known as the biggest subsidiary lake of Biwa Lake. But it is only a small part of the original lagoon area including former Dainakako, Shonakako, Nishinoko and others. During the 20th century, wetlands and subsidiary lakes around Lake Biwa have been reclaimed in the name of safety and productivity, as mentioned already. This was also the case for Nishinoko's lagoon area: more than 90 percent of the original lagoon area was converted into rice fields. But Nishinoko alone was different from others: people could save the subsidiary lake from modern engineered interventions. It could survive because the landowners rejected governmental expropriation and that is the reason why the wetlands and reed beds can still be found around Nishinoko. For the same reason villages around the wetlands of the subsidiary lake still keep their traditional reeds festivals.

Taimatsu (torch) for festival

KAWASHIMA Fumiya and FURTER Tobias chose Lake Nishinoko as their site for research and design. They both proposed distinctive wooden pile structures at multiple locations surrounding the subsidiary lake. While KAWASHIMA Fumiya chose "reed cycle" as his subject for his project, FURTER Tobias picked a "unity of the circle". KAWASHIMA Fumiya's three structures visualise the cycle of the reeds from harvesting to the festival fire: firstly, a reed drying and storage area; secondly, a reed tying area (totem-making area); and thirdly, a meeting and starting point for the festival. The components of FURTER's design are focused more on daily activities and usage such as a promenade and viewpoints. Both projects praise the festival's behind-the-scenes preparation places and phases (Ke) throughout the year and sublimate them into distinctive events (Hare).

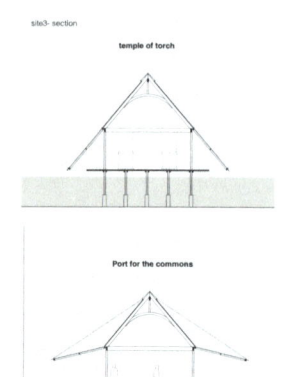

KAWASHIMA Fumiya: Build a common void in Lake Nishinoko

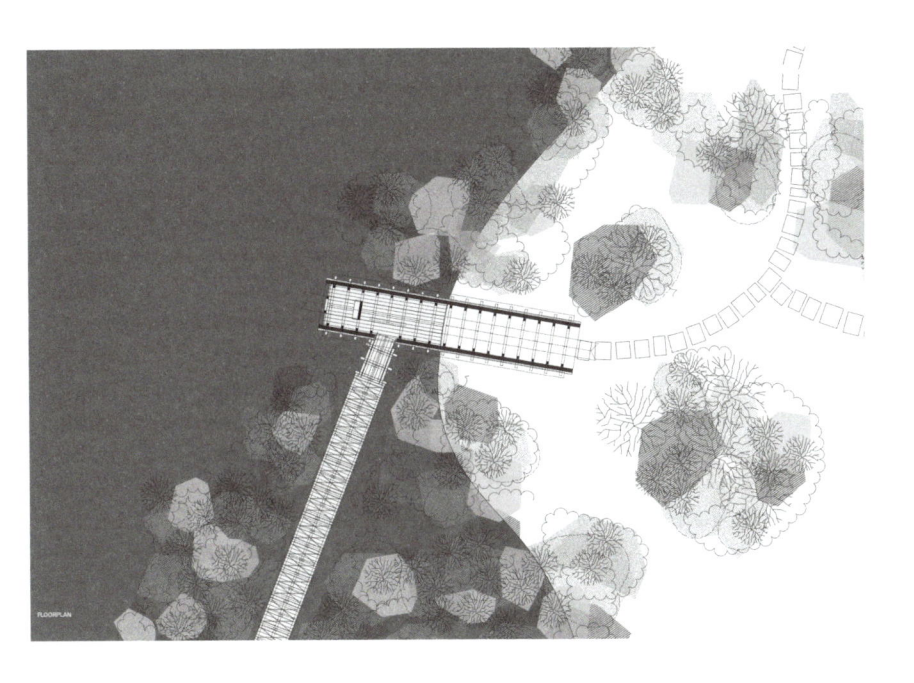

FLOORPLAN

FURTER Tobias: Build a
common void in Lake Nishinoko

STONE AND WATER

ROSSMAIER Lando

RITUAL AND HABIT

The extensive dialogue of last semester brought the KIT and us from the productive common ground to the rituals whose loss we regretted. We wanted to trace the vanishing collective knowledge and renew it. Today, after reading Byung-Chul Han,[1] I understand rituals as Ge*wohn*heiten (habit[ation]s), as a house in which we feel protected. We share joy and suffering in them. With rituals we not only confront our fears, as with a lullaby, but equally convey common meaning and belonging. Thus, they serve as a container for memory.

The Ise Shrine, probably the world's most famous example of a place of remembrance, has been completely rebuilt around 62 times over 1300 years. The rhythm of dismantling and replacing is nearly a generation, that is 20 years. To me as a foreign observer, this process shed new light on architectonic permanence as I had understood it. This constant renewal keeps the memory alive over the unbelievable temporal dimension of 1300 years. The shrine was presumably originally intended to store provisions in case of famine. From early on, even before the wood construction of the storeroom would weather over the years, an identical replacement was standing ready. A pragmatic precautionary measure thus turned into a rite laden with significance. The threat of hunger was eliminated, and a nearly identical process passed down over umpteen generations was turned into a transcendent category that points beyond it: eternity.

On the wings of the wind
the voice of the stream . .
The conversation of the waves
on the breath of the night . .
My little alarm clock is ticking . .
O time and eternity![2]

[1] Byung-Chul Han: *The Disappearance of Rituals. A Topology of the Present,* trans. Daniel Steuer, Cambridge 2021.
[2] O Zeit und Ewigkeit! by the German poet and writer Christian Morgenstern (1871–1914).

Water & Danger	Lake Lucerne	Hazard Map
	Lake Biwa	Hazard Map
Water & Beauty	Lake Lucerne	Hidden Beauty
	Lake Biwa	Eight Views of Ōmi
Water & Commons	Lake Lucerne	Productivity
	Lake Biwa	Ritual
Water & Eternity	Lake Lucerne	Stone
	Lake Biwa	Re-Metabolism

MEASURING THE INFINITE

Eternity can be explained by its opposite: transience. Eternity should not be confused with infinity, which we understand as limitlessness, as a borderless, endless something, like the expanses of the universe. For a worm, a meadow is already infinite, for me the sea is. Humanity has since time immemorial seemed predestined to overcome limits. When searching for galactic boundaries, physicists have to proceed as if in a forest in which trees block the view of the edge of the forest. Using satellites, they send increasingly sensitive optical instruments into space and hope for a better position in order to make out through the countless heaps of stars and galaxies — not fog! — the edge by means of light shifting from red to violet. It was determined that our cosmos is — and hence we too are — precisely 13.81 billion years old. Since the Big Bang, the universe has been expanding in all directions with incredible speed, like a giant explosion. That is why no edges can be found. Some experts believe that the seam of the universe is like a very curly edge of a gigantic kale leaf. In its infinite curves, time and space bend. We cannot perceive or understand this but we can calculate it. But the abstract, mathematical approach only makes it harder to understand reality. We have long been reading science fiction about space-time shortcuts and time machines, it still goes far beyond our imagination. What we might happen upon way out in the universe, beyond the last visible light from a star, beyond that and still farther, even farther beyond that and still farther, much farther than beyond everything and infinitely farther …, that escapes our finite, causal thought system. We want to but cannot ever get beyond that.

NOT BEYOND THAT. LIMITED.

At the Kunsthaus Zurich I entered a room by Olafur Eliasson. In it, spotlights pointed horizontally reflected, in the otherwise impenetrable fog, the light as a focused level above the visitors. It created the impression that there was a surface of water lying above me that was infused with the most delicate particles. The reflections looked like an atmospheric transition, from a layer of water to a layer of gas or air above it. It was like being a fish in an aquarium. With this change in perspective, I had a sense of our limitedness, of how narrow the range of our senses is and of how much we are bound to the wafer-thin atmosphere of earth. Although fish sometimes catch air outside of their element, they ultimately remain captive by the water. Only a few hundred thousand years of evolution could change that.

And us? Despite all the efforts of astrophysics, despite the very recent tourist trips into space and the associated, still unresolved conflicts about to whom this universe really belongs, we really know very little. Only thanks to technical

Olafur Eliasson, *Symbotic Seeing*, Kunsthaus Zurich, 2020
Photo by ROSSMAIER Lando

achievements can we survive outside the earth. And it is all the more frightening, when the paradox of supposedly unlimited growth and simultaneous limitation leads us to our own planet's ruin.[3] Because of such limitations on infinity, our big questions always end up, a priori with a kind of unconditional precondition. Relativities necessarily end up in the absolute. Depending on a spiritual inclination, we conceive of something between singularity and creation. Unimaginability brings us somewhat closer to eternity, but it becomes a dead end.

SPIRITUAL SPACE

In an interview with the philosopher Joachim Kirchhoff,[4] the interviewer laments that astronomers, just like financial jugglers, are driven by infinite columns of numbers. Perhaps. Both professions, in any case, only allegedly achieve control with their limitless rows of numbers, because at the same time reality becomes unduly abstract and distanced from us. At present, we seem to be separated from reality all too often. Some "bend" it into alternative realities. Perhaps we find it so difficult, for well-known reasons, to reorient our world, because our relationship to it has suffered, and because we no longer experience the effects of our action directly.[5] If we misunderstand infinity, only intellectual space – not existential space – is accessible, according to Kirchhoff. We can better enter existential, cosmologically alive space by way of music, dance, observing nature, seeing natural connections, in essence by way of spiritual experiences, which hopefully include architectonic and spatial ones.

INTRA RATHER THAN INTER

The French philosopher François Jullien comes to a similar conclusion in his collection of essays *"Living off Landscape"*[6] but by a very different route. He recommends that we stop regarding the landscape as a picture, a static vis-à-vis, but instead experience its liveliness as a holistic effect. He believes, that this becomes discernible by means of physical perception in movement, not from an elevated viewpoint, but only by roaming through it. In the sense of: here I hear the murmuring of a stream, there is a gentle hollow, up there lies a moss-covered field of scree with a fox's lair, and above that, a field crisscrossed by the fine lines of high-tension wires. Landscape thus becomes a living admixture, a milieu, in which living conditions and living creatures affect each other, in both directions.[7]

Jullien translates "paysage" with the Chinese words for "stone" and "water". The Chinese reading of landscape reinterprets the European convention. It frames landscape as something lying in between, something that cannot be pinned down. There is no objectifying of landscape, no longer any silent object

[3] In search of a new master narrative in "Sternstunde der Philosophie" on May 5, 2021 with Philipp Blom, https://youtu.be/VhRbFA53He8?si=6dQirtExHVVIEM_r

[4] Joachim Kirchhoff: "Das Unendliche und das Endliche", YouTube, April 19, 2021.

[5] See Lando Rossmaier about how human psyche is separated from our natural habitat "Die Moderne", https://rossmaier.com/joomla/forschungalehre/30-essays/134-die-moderne.html

[6] François Jullien: *Living off Landscape; or, The Unthought-Of in Reason*, trans. Pedro Rodríguez, Lanham 2018.

[7] Bruno Latour: *Facing Gaia, Eight Lectures on the New Climatic Regime*, trans. Catherine Porter, Cambridge 2017, is based on James Lovelock's ideas from 1972.

in the eye of the beholder, but rather an infinitely rich area of tension in the middle of the antonyms of brusque and gentle, flat and steep, etc. I find this way of thinking stimulating, because it keeps the concept of landscape undefined. It can therefore be and become many things, including the artificial landscape of infrastructure buildings – and the living creatures in them. And thus, out of an elemental osmotic pair of concepts, emerges a poetic landscape cosmos: stone and water, water and stone. Moss – life follows.

FALLING APART AND BUILDING

Ruined barn bases, in Val Bavone in the canton of Ticino, merged back into the soil from which they were once lifted. In a project by Martino Pedrozzi, with students at the Accademia in Mendrisio, the chunks of stone lying around were stacked up again to form sharp rectangles, but in a few decades they will have collapsed again.

When planning, I strive to work with local materials and consider future maintenance, but I have only lately begun to consider deconstruction and reconstruction as well as local cycles. For a long period of time, I was used to not understanding construction as a mere phase, but believed, with a mistaken understanding of eternity, that buildings could be completely finished. Yet buildings, that are not affected by time, do not exist – and are not needed. Using durable constructions and structures to harmonise buildings with the natural rhythms of resource extraction, in order to achieve a balance between structural and natural production, ought to be the basis for all of us. In future, we would better see building as a form of maintenance rather than production. Eternity would be perceived more correctly: Instead of progress, an act of reconstruction synchronised with the pace of nature.

NEGATING TIME, PERMANENCE, SILENCE

Permanence, the European notion of defiant resistance, to the threat of transience, manifests itself particularly vividly, when man-made order and Cartesian precision threaten to dissolve into natural chaos. I am reminded of Piranesian drawings with scenes like excavation sites. Untamed plant growth clutters the buildings. Stone drums, the remains of timberwork and other fragments lie between sprawling bushes. What was once carefully erected is falling to the ground again. The gravity stored in the carefully stacked stones is released in the collapse. Few remnants remain – for now, they too will fall.

In Louis Kahn's works, such a ruin-like expression acts as a supporting idea. Windows are missing or are hidden by shadows, deep in the wall. The foreground is characterised by the archaism and pathos of the exposed walls. "Brut"

(French for raw), without any covering plaster or slurry, they were built piece by piece. They are what they are. Present.

In a highly esteemed lecture at the ETH, entitled "Silence and Light",[8] Kahn subsumed his universal desire for timelessness within ambiguity. He called it the spiritual "eternal present". His rooms are built without distraction, reduced to a few natural materials, visible and direct. Light and shadow, which for him can certainly be understood as a building material, evoke the poetry of the heavy, calm brick or concrete walls. The course of the sun and stars set the mood for his spaces. Light, dark, space and emptiness. The omissions lead to an essentialisation. By dispensing with any triviality, the use of universal geometries and a reduced architectural language, indications of a construction period become illegible. The building seems to have fallen out of time, silent, but eternal?

The contrast of the buildings to the time-bound world, to living nature, including us humans, is intensified by the created essence. On the one hand, the presence of the stoic building and, on the other, the fact, that we are thrown back on ourselves, or even more clearly, a permanent edifice, that has fallen out of time in the view of a life that is now all the more volatile and certainly finite. When the initial awe of the sublime building fades, a strong echo emerges. We question the relationship between ourselves, our meaningfulness, and the building conceived for "eternity", including its cultural and symbolic dimension. With the inkling of leaving one day, we introspect, become silent, possibly sensing that it is not the monument itself, but our differentness to it, the deeply moving tension that lies within it.

TWO PROJECTS

Such an experience does not always require the use of grand architecture. It can also be discovered on a bench, during a hike, while gazing into the landscape. Two student projects are picked out to illustrate this:

Between the Mediterranean hamlet of Bauen and the village of Isleten on Urnersee, which is exposed to strong foehn winds, the student ROMA GÓMEZ Blanca opens up the buried tunnel sections of an existing gallery. She supports the tunnel vault and makes the path passable again. In a convincing way, she succeeds in creating a dialogue, between the natural and the man-made by means of nuanced paving and furniture made of natural stone, similar to Pikioni's work near the Acropolis. It modifies the perception of space and strengthens the effect of the craggy rock vaults. New spatial configurations mediate between the mountain massif and the lake, between the intimate, cooling gallery and the veduta-like views across the lake, over to the other side and to the mountains beyond. Bays, basins, islands, embankments, tongues, patches are her

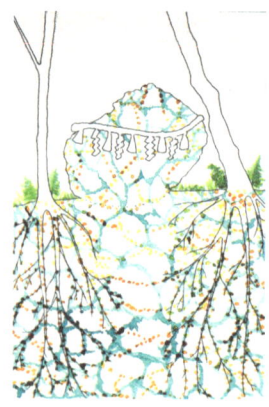

NAITOU Sari: Eternal network in Isleten

[8] *Louis I. Kahn – Silence and Light, The Lecture at ETH Zurich, February 12, 1969, Zurich 2013.*

vocabulary. The chain is interspersed with rocky niches designed for larger groups. She is by no means interested in spectacular bathing spots and barbecue areas. Rather, ROMA GÓMEZ Blanca reveals subtle references to the beauty of the relationship between the supposed permanence of the rock – the slope crumbles and the tunnels do not last forever – and the changeable lake, between constant stone and unstable water. The work draws attention to the "in-between".

Similar, but wonderfully different, was her Japanese colleague NAITOU Sari's idea of Isleten. The shallow delta of the Isenthal stream is now a wasteland of a bygone timber and explosives industry. What remains is a harbour, manufacturers' villas and trees. Today the place looks desolate. NAITOU Sari claims, what I have not been able to verify, but which I am keen to believe: Megaliths, i.e., large stones, have a positive influence on the quality of the soil beneath them. They interact with the soil, the hyphae of the fungal mycelia grow into the stone pores, which become larger over time. New veins of water would emerge under the boulders. Minerals would enrich the soil. According to Sari's animistic view, her understanding of eternity is represented neither by the newly placed megaliths nor the water, but solely by their interaction – without humans. She consistently declares Isleten to be a prohibited zone to humans in the future, an untouchable, sacred empty space. She proposes to remove the abandoned houses and sealed surfaces, to close the roads towards Bauen and to open up the ground for springs and streams. Finally, she places stop stones set with strings, so-called Sekimori-Ishi, which now mark a zone that will be left to itself for centuries. The area is now an inaccessible reserve – with a magic protection spell.

THE OTHER

Unexpectedly, both authors do not formulate an architectural answer, but instead they aim at preserving the landscape, at what must change, for it to become what is already inherent. Their notion of eternity is not described by everlasting or sublime objects, but by a resonance[9] in the topos. It is about the fugue opened in the interaction, the inexplicable void. This is all the more pleasing because many architects still seem to be satisfied with just a beautiful object.

This insight prompts me to conclude my previous considerations with a philosophical approach that could even be taken as a valid way of seeing and working for our future. Emmanuel Lévinas, a French-Lithuanian philosopher, outlines it with the concept of the "visage", which I understand as an ethical responsibility towards the other. Our approach to the world is determined less

[9] cf. Hartmut Rosa's concept of resonance and the unavailability that it requires, in *Resonanz: Eine Soziologie der Weltbeziehung*, Berlin 2019.

by thinking or consciousness than by our relationship to this other. He emphasises, that the other confronts us as a unique individual with their own needs,
suffering and vulnerability. This encounter with the other triggers an ethical
responsibility in us, which consists of turning towards otherness, listening to it
and recognising it in its uniqueness. In this way, self-forgetfulness overcomes our
own ego and self-centredness. The well-being and needs of the other are placed
above our own.

Lévinas argues: Ethical responsibility is a fundamental, non-negotiable obliga-
tion, that shapes our relationships with others. I would like to expand as follows:
"…it shapes our relationship to the world as architects" and thus makes cli-
mate-friendly construction a given. But this perspective is even more far-reaching: We should become aware of the fact, that we hope to always create reso-
nant relationships in our profession. Basically, we who create space are
"relationship workers" who, just like the mentioned students, now bring not just
stone and water, but material – both in the sense of substance and as content
– into a meaningful interrelation within constructions.

We construct a social fabric with our houses, their inhabitants and the open
spaces. By choosing the building material, we influence its extraction and its
return into the cycle. The more far-reaching, holistic and dense our relationships
are,[10] the more robust and sustainable such a "weave of significance" becomes.
This woven fabric interacts multi-laterally and is supported in many ways, resist-
ant to light-hearted ideas.

The semester focus "Eternity", which I reinterpreted as stone and water,
drew our attention to the care with which we point beyond ourselves. In caring
for the other, we inevitably find ourselves in the moment, in the smallest part
of eternity. In the activity of caring for the other, the future and the past both
recede into the background. In a similar way to how we breathe in meditations
or seek to experience presence and timelessness in other ritual practices by
performing shared actions.

We might counter the omnipresent fragmentation and separation with a
kind of "resonance machines".[11] We are not isolated individuals, but we are part
of a self-regenerating whole and its inherent rhythms. This became all the more
striking as we gradually understood that, in an animistic view, there is no difference between material and spiritual existence. Everything is essential.[12] In our
involvement, we establish connections, allow closeness and transcend ourselves.
The different conception of eternity, that we gained in the exchange with our
Japanese colleagues, might provide a key to creating works, that will genuinely
persist.

[10] The German word "wirken" means both to have an effect and to weave or knit, related to weaved fabric (Wirkware), fulling (Walken), felting (Filzen). On other occasions, I have pointed out the etymological relationship in German, cf. "Sinngeflechte" in *Feine Fassaden – Tektonik Schweizer Stadthäuser*, Karin Ohashi and Lando Rossmaier (Eds.), HSLU Luzern 2022.

[11] Shinohara's "space machine" in the Tanikawa House may serve as a reference to empty space. See. Tibor Joanelly: *Shinoharistics. An Essay about a House*, Zurich 2020.

[12] Lando Rossmaier: "Zweischneidig", March 7, 2022. https://www.rossmaier.com/joomla/texte-liste/30-essays/163-zweischneidig

ROMA GÓMEZ Blanca: In between the floor and the ground, in the tunnel between Bauen and Isleten

FORM, EMPTINESS, ETERNITY

SUN BUSCHOR Mulan

廬山煙雨浙江潮
未至千般恨不消
到得還來別無事
廬山煙雨浙江潮

蘇軾

Mount Lu in misty rain; the River Che at high tide.
When I had not been there, no rest from the pain of longing!
I went and I returned. That is all.
Mount Lu in misty rain; the River Che at high tide.

Su Shi[1]

The last semester of the five-year joint project was not only a conclusion but also a new beginning. During the term we continued to explore Water and Eternity through investigating the phenomenon of metabolism. From a biological point of view, metabolism explains the chemical changes that take place in a cell or an organism. These changes provide energy and the materials which cells and organisms need to grow, reproduce and move to sustain life.[2] But also, the original Chinese/Japanese version of the word, Shinchintaisha 新陳代謝, has overtones of a spiritual perspective, very similar to the Buddhist concept of impermanence, the meaning of renewal, replacement and regeneration. Metabolism brings the possibility of eternity in a dynamic way to the creatures of this world, not only from the biological perspective, but also from a spiritual perspective. We do not know whether nor how and where Eternity exists. Moreover, eternity not only points to the future, but also exists in the present and can even be sought in the part. Architecture should coexist with time. Therefore, the focus of this last semester was the application of the concept of transiency or change in architectural research and design, as every change is a fundamental truth about existence.

[1] Su Shi, 1037-1101, was a Chinese poet, essayist, calligrapher, painter, and scholar-official who lived during the Song dynasty.
[2] "Metabolism". https://en.wikipedia.org/wiki/metabolism

Water & Danger	Lake Lucerne	Hazard Map
	Lake Biwa	Hazard Map
Water & Beauty	Lake Lucerne	Hidden Beauty
	Lake Biwa	Eight Views of Ōmi
Water & Commons	Lake Lucerne	Productivity
	Lake Biwa	Ritual
Water & Eternity	Lake Lucerne	Stone
	Lake Biwa	Re-Metabolism

LIFE HAS MANY FORMS

Cloud, tsunami, rain, snow, hail... Water has many forms. Through the five years of research, fieldwork, design exercises, critique etc. we have also created a good "form" for this project. Form is not a way of expression, but a connotation that keeps the tradition alive. Thus, the Culture of Water can also be transformed into other forms. One of the important research methods of our project was the comparative study of the two lakes, through which we could better understand their significance. We started on similarities, moved into differences and diversities and finally returned to similarities. Over these five years, I stood at Lake Lucerne and Lake Biwa countless times. As time goes by, for me, the differences between the East and the West dissolved; no difference between coming and going, there is no dualism.

"The bodies of the caterpillar and butterfly have nothing in common and they do not share the same world: one crawls on the ground and the other flutters its wings in the air. And yet they are one and the same life. […] All living creatures are, in a certain sense, the same body, the same life and the same self, continually passing from form to form, from subject to subject, from existence to existence. […] Difference is never a nature; it is a destiny and a task. We have no choice but to become different, we are obliged to metamorphose."[3]

[3] Emanuele Coccia: *Metamorphoses,* Cambridge and Oxford 2021

Sunset of Lake Lucerne, photography by SUN BUSCHOR Mulan, 2024

FORM IS EXACTLY EMPTINESS; EMPTINESS IS EXACTLY FORM

This excerpt from the "Heart Sutra" always reminds me of visiting the artwork of the German artist Wolfgang Laib in Bündner Kunstmuseum Chur. "Crossing the River" was the title of the exhibition. The temporary installation was in a laid-out field of thousands of rice mounds. It was a very simple form, causing a feeling of emptiness. At one end of the "rice field" was a small mound of colourful pollen and at the other end a eucharist casket. Wolfgang Laib creates an astonishing relationship between "this shore" and "the other shore". Our life can be seen as crossing the river. To reach the other shore with each step of the crossing is the way of true living. And the most important thing is to express your true nature in the simplest, most adequate way and to appreciate it in the smallest existence. By working with natural materials such as pollen, rice, milk or bees wax, Wolfgang Laib recognises that we are part of a much larger and interconnected form of life. In his work, he connects everything in the micro and macro worlds; life and death, transience and eternity, form and emptiness. His love and devotion to the raw materials he uses to transcend the physical. From the ephemeral to the eternal, his work magnifies the natural world and the universe, encouraging us to abandon our selfish view of the humans as static and independent to nature. By reawakening our critical thinking, it gives us the hope of repairing or rebuilding the relationship between humans and nature.

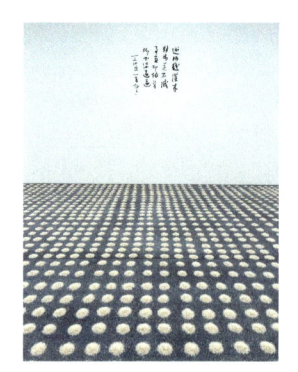

Wolfgang Laib, Exhibition "Crossing the River" Bündner Kunstmuseum, Chur 2022

"If you paint a picture, the picture becomes yours. If I gather pollen or pour milk onto a stone, what I get is not a painting that is mine, because I didn't make it and it's not about me, but about a universal idea of the world. I collect pollen, which represents the beginning of plant life and has incredible power, like the sky or the sun. But, like pollen, the sky and sun aren't mine. I'm only a participant in the absolute beauty of all this […]. This time has come to change our culture, to look beyond the individual and see something much bigger."[4]

WASTE MANAGEMENT IN BRUNNEN

HAMAIE Mari proposed a new topography made from construction waste soil for the existing park on the lakeside in Brunnen. Using fixed anchor pins, the soil can be stabilised and hardened, in order to create a pit for biodegradable bags. People who live in Brunnen will participate in this new system of waste management. One biodegradable composting bag will be distributed to each household for composting food scraps. On a certain day of the week, the government will collect the compost and deposit the bag at the site. The bag and its content will then decompose within three to six months. In this system, people are not the only participants. Bugs, insects and small animals will be attracted. The birds come to eat the insects. They defecate and new plants and trees sprout. Trees

[4] Maria Grazia Marini (Ed.): *Wolfgang Laib at Sant' Apollinare in Classe*, exhibition catalogue, Ravenna 2014, Turin 2016

and plants grow, providing a habitat for insects and birds. Residents take care of the plants and trees in the park. Rather than planting new vegetation, a garden emerges from seeds carried by birds and the wind. In this project, HAMAIE Mari positioned herself not as a top-down architect or landscape designer, but as a gardener who observes, cares and cultivates the natural ecosystem of the garden. Her proposal is an environmental manifesto, which posits that the natural world and humankind cannot be understood as separate from one another. In this sense, we should think of the entire planet as a garden, and ourselves as gardeners and its keepers, not as owners, responsible for the care of the complexity and diversity of life.

TEMPLE OF WATER IN CHIKUBUSHIMA

Chikubushima 竹生島 is an island located in the northem part of Lake Biwa. Chikubushima has long upheld its ancient historical legacy as a spiritual setting.

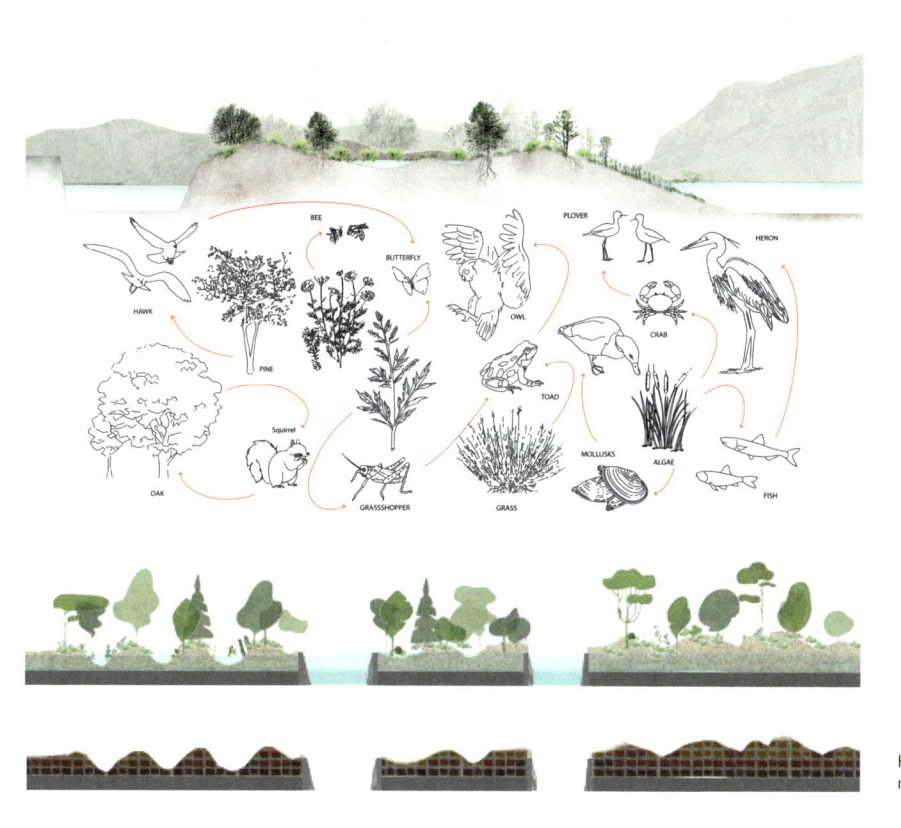

HAMAIE Mari: Waste management in Brunnen

Despite Lake Biwa being the sacred water source, it is widely used for various needs: agriculture, fishing, transportation, etc. As explained in the interview, it also suffers from water skiing. In Chikubushima, the lake water is primarily used in rituals, purified for drinking and serves for hygienic needs. The stream starts from the lowest point in the harbour, where the lake water is pumped and stored in tanks. It will be used as a starting point in the project proposal of SHEGAY Alina for the Temple of Water. From the mountain down to the lake, the route of prayers and the water way are merged into one. The water follows up the hill by the existing pipeline and flows down through plant-based water filtration. It is a sustainable method for cleaning water by using plants in aquatic systems, absorbing nutrients, bacteria, metals, and chemicals. For instance moss, pine tree, water mint, water lilies and iris. The worshipper can see it in the small forms with special plants near the road, where the water is guided to its destination. "Temple of Water" is a place where we gather to participate in a ritual, using purified water. Water can be felt in various forms here: by seeing, hearing, smelling, tasting, touching, before its return to the initial source – back into the Lake, the emptiness. The landscape and architecture design have completed an eternal cycle of receiving and giving.

THE WATERFALL
"If you go to Japan and visit Eiheiji 永平寺 monastery, just before you enter you will see a small bridge called Hanshaku-kyo 半杓橋, which means "Half- Dipper Bridge." Whenever Dogen-zenji dipped water from the river, he used only half a dipperful, returning the rest to the river again, without throwing it away. That is why we call the bridge Hanshaku-kyo, "Half-Dipper Bridge." […] It takes time, a long time, for the water to finally reach the bottom of the waterfall. And it seems to me that our human life may be like this. […] Before we were born we had no feeling; we were one with the universe. After we are separated by birth from this oneness, as the water falling from the waterfall is separated by the wind and rocks, then we have feeling. You have difficulty because you have feeling. You attach to the feeling you have without knowing just how this kind of feeling is created. When you do not realize that you are one with the river, or one with the universe, you have fear. Whether it is separated into drops or not, water is water. Our life and death are the same thing. […] When the water returns to its original oneness with the river, it no longer has any individual feeling to it; it resumes its own nature, and finds composure. How very glad the water must be to come back to the original river! If this is so, what feeling will we have when we die? I think we are like the water in the dipper."[4]

[4] Zen Mind, Beginner's Mind by Suzuki Shunryu

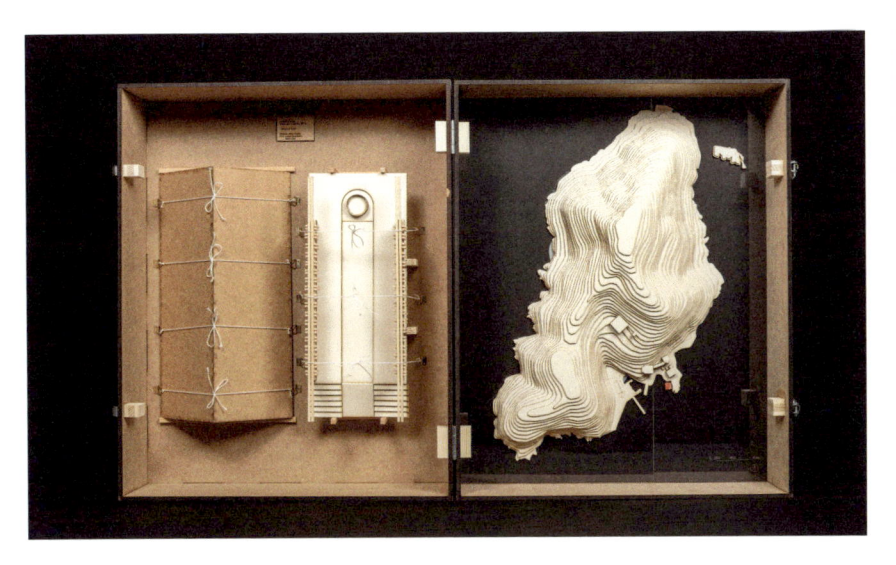

SHEGAY Alina:
Temple of Water in
Chikubushima

Waterdipper at the tea
ceremony, Kyoto, 1951, by
Werner Bischof.
This photograph shows the
Grand Master Sen Sōshitsu XIV
(Tantansai) of the Japanese tea
ceremony school (Urasenke),
placing a bamboo ladle on a pot
of boiling water.

TWO CULTURES – THE PAST
ふたつの文化 – その過去

THOMSEN Hans Bjarne

LAKES THROUGH WORDS AND IMAGES

Across time and cultures, large lakes continue to engage the imagination of artists and poets. The Biwa Lake in Japan and the Vierwaldstättersee in Switzerland are both large bodies of water, located next to towering mountains. Like miniature oceans, these lakes evoke diverse imagery in the arts, from the more culturally determined to the more universal.

Atmospheric views that describe specific moments in the day on the lakes tend to be features of artistic works – whether in sunlight, during a storm or in the early dawn or late evening. For example, we may look at the famous *Eight Views of Ōmi Province* 近江八景 by Utagawa Hiroshige 歌川広重 (1797–1868). Hiroshige was deeply engaged by the subjectand produced almost 20 series in his lifetime. Looking at the *Autumn Moon at Ishiyama* 石山秋月 from his early series of 1832 we can see how the artist has selected a bird's-eye perspective to show a particular point in time: the moment at dusk where the daylight in the distance changes into night; darkness descends on the upper cliffs of the Ishiyama Mountain and there is a full autumn moon above. Looking at this depiction as well as the other prints in the series, we can discern how Hiroshige combines three elements – the lake, the mountains and the sky – all three of which are given central roles in the print.

In Switzerland, the Vierwaldstättersee is often depicted in the works of artists with a similar consciousness for atmosphere; in this case, more often in oil on canvas paintings than the woodblock print technique typical for Japan.

Looking at a representative Swiss work, the *Vierwaldstättersee* by Willy F. Burger (1882–1964), we see a scenery from the perspective of the lake – a low viewpoint looking towards the sky that emphasises the sheer mass of the mountains. There are points of similarity with Hiroshige's print, such as the three elements we already distinguished. They also become the focus in Burger's painting: the lake, the mountains and the sky with its distinctive cotton clouds. Unlike Hiroshige's series which show a populated landscape, with houses, bridges, temples and fishermen in their boats, here there are no traces of humans: it is all

Photo by BECK Jürgen

majestic nature. There is a certain timelessness, as if the scene had been re-moved from history. With the artist's eye, we perceive nature as powerful and monumental, representing a very different world than that inhabited by human beings.

If one considers the treatment of the motif of the lake by poets, there are further interesting points of comparison between the two cultures. As for Lake Biwa, the by far most famous example is the set of eight poems composed by Prince Konoe Masaie 近衛政家 (1444–1505) and his son, Prince Hisamichi 近衛尚通 (1472–1544), in the 15–16th centuries. These poems were based on a much older Chinese tradition, the *Eight Views of Xiaoxiang* which were created in both poems and paintings during the 11th century. While this tradition referred to the region of the Xiaoxiang, with its two large rivers, the Japanese poets transport-ed the theme to Lake Biwa, starting a long-lasting tradition that became popular with Japanese artists, most notably Hiroshige. Much like the way the prints depict them, the poems describe the times of the day and natural phenomena as well as humans and their habitations.

The poem from this poetry cycle describing this particular view is also writ-ten in a cartouche on the print:

Autumn Moon at Ishiyama

Ah, Ishiyama mountain –
Could even the moonlit
Akashi or Suma match
your view of the
shining dabchick ocean?

Here the poets compare the view from Ishiyama with two other famous sites in Japan that were often visited and appear repeatedly in classical Japanese po-etry: Akashi and Suma, both located near the ocean and providing poetic views that reverberated through Japanese literature and were celebrated in countless poems through the centuries. In the poem Ishiyama is in effect placing the splen-did view over Lake Biwa into contexts that would have been intimately known by the cultured elite. Japanese culture often functions through hints rather than directness and so it is here, as Lake Biwa is mentioned as the "dabchick ocean," the dabchick or lesser grebe (in Japanese "nio" 鳰), a duck that swims in these waters – again, a name that often appears in classical Japanese poetry, where the dabchick ocean become a poetry name for Lake Biwa. In other words, the poem places the location and the lake within a longer literary tradition.

When we study the poems inspired by the Vierwaldstättersee, we find both similarities and contrasts. The atmospheric variations, seasons and natural scenery are described just as in the Japanese poems, yet there is another element. In the "Vom Vierwaldstättersee – I, II" poem by Jacob Burckhardt (1818–1897) from his collection *Ferien, Eine Herbstgabe*, we see phrases that are reminiscent of Hiroshige's prints as well as Burger's painting, such as:

Rosenwolken ziehn einher,
Feuriger, dann wieder blässer;
In der Tiefe fluten sie,
Zart gespiegelt vom Gewässer.

Such phrases describe the poetry of the natural forces of the lake. We become aware of the celebration of nature in all its colourful glory, not only on the lake, but also on the shores nearby:

Unter kühlen Walnussschatten
Schlängeln sich die leichten Pfade
Grünumhegt, durch Blumenwiesen
An des blauen See's Gestade

Yet there are other factors as well. Karl May (1842–1912) described his encounter with the lake in his poem "Am Vierwaldstätter See".

Der Abend küßte grad die nacht
Bei heilig ernstem Sternenleuchten,
    Da hab ich mich noch aufgemacht,
Mir Herz und Stirne zu befeuchten.
Die Gierigkeit der mammonsklaven
    War mir so leid, that mir so weh;
Das Auge schloß sich nicht zum Schlafen;
    Drum ging hinaus ich an den See.

Er lag so still; er lag so hehr
In Fels und Matten eingebettet,
    Als hätte, so wie ich, auch er
Sich aus der Welt hierhergerettet.

These lines are interesting for a number of reasons. They again portray nature as a place separate from the human world – and as a powerful realm that has certain restorative powers. It is cast as a world in direct opposition to the sphere of humans and imbued with a potential to remedy the degrading effect of the human world – here described as living like slaves to the world of mammon. In short, nature is ascribed a Rousseau-like purity, strength and an ability for cleansing the corruption of the human world. Moreover, in contrast to the volatility and change of the human world, it has an eternal value and represents a realm that is ever constant.

If we consider the Japanese words and images, we observe a very different view of nature. Here, nature is represented as being in a harmony with the human world. There is an interconnectedness between the worlds of nature and humans, as exemplified in the daily endeavours of the people living around or working on the lake. Constructed objects, such as villages, temples and bridges, punctuate the scene and even – in the case of bridges – cross the lake, thus, in effect, controlling it.

On the print *Autumn Moon at Ishiyama* by Hiroshige, we see a large temple on the Ishiyama Mountain, as well as a village at its foot. Further away, a long bridge crosses the lake. While we also sense the wilderness in the depiction of the mountain, this is, at the same time, a nature that accommodates human beings.

Nor do the scenes by Hiroshige represent an idealised eternal and unchanging nature, as his art is very much bound to human history. First of all, Song-dynasty China is evoked by the use of the eight poems subsequently transferred to Japan, as described before. Yet there are additional ties to history and culture. The tacit hint by Hiroshige to Murasaki Shikibu, lady-in-waiting at the Imperial court, in describing Ishiyama under the autumn moon, will likely have been understood by most of Hiroshige's contemporaries.

Murasaki Shikibu 紫式部 (c. 973 – c. 1014 or 1025) is famous as the author of the world's first novel, the Tales of Prince Genji 源氏物語, composed around the year 1000. A legend states that Murasaki began writing her novel while viewing the autumn moon over Lake Biwa during a stay at the Buddhist temple Ishiyamadera 石山寺. Hiroshige has clearly placed this temple on Ishiyama Mountain, with the full moon above; in this way, the reference to Murasaki and the Tales of Prince Genji are unmistakable. Another connection is to the two sites mentioned in the poem: both Suma and Akashi are names of chapters within the *Tale of Genji*.

The bridge, too, has a deeper cultural and historical meaning. The Chinese Bridge of Seta 瀬田唐橋 seen in the print was considered to be one of the three great bridges of Japan; it was originally constructed in the 7th century and appears in the earliest Japanese histories. It became the centre of numerous famous battles and was repeatedly burned down and rebuilt. The bridge was also on the major route that connected Kyoto with the new capital of Japan, Edo. In this way, the bridge in Hiroshige's print was a famous location in the history of Japan, as well as a site that often appears in its art and literature.

In other words, Hiroshige's print of the *Autumn Moon at Ishiyama* shows Lake Biwa as being not only embedded into the lives of human beings, but also deeply intertwined with the culture and history of Japan.

Looking at the comparisons above, we may say that there are, to some extent, similar ways of thinking about the nature of large lakes in both cultures – as scenic places that embody the intersection between land, water and the sky. However, there are also significant differences. In the west, the Vierwaldstättersee is described as a majestic and powerful place where an eternal, unchanging nature epitomises a world separate from the human world. It is in some ways diametrically opposed to the human realm, as in its ability to mitigate corruptive human influences. Lake Biwa, by contrast, stands for a place characterised by a fundamental interrelationship of nature with humans, their work and their habitat. Moreover, it is a place that has been shaped by the events of human history and culture. Although the two large lakes are similar in their form and location in the mountain landscapes, their cultural context has created a very different perception of them in the human imagination.

Autumn Moon at Ishiyama
石山秋月 by Utagawa Hiroshige
歌川広重
1832

Vierwaldstättersee – Lake Lucerne
by Willy F. Burger
1941

ONE WATER – FOUR VIEWS
一水四見

GEISSBÜHLER Dieter
SUN BUSCHOR Mulan

THE TERRITORY AS A PALIMPSEST[1]

Based on André Corboz's metaphor of reading the territory as a palimpsest, i.e. as a "skin" on which several texts are not only superimposed, but where each new text is influenced by its "scraped off" predecessor, the aim for the first semester was to reapply a text in the sense of speculative research. Although parts of the previous text are erased to make room for the new one, visible traces nevertheless still inform the essence of the new text.

The territory, in this specific case the two lakes in the regions of Kyoto and Lucerne, is understood as a territorial unit, but the investigation is looking for the existing nuances. As reservoirs of cultural appropriation over time and through different social influences, they become archaeological sites with the objective of attributing a new existence to the finds.

The overarching starting point in the first semester was the joint investigation of the connection between forms of life and the conditions of the inhabited landscape that shape existence. This was intended to lay the foundation for further research in the five-year collaboration between the KIT and HSLU and thus define a multi-layered approach to analytical and design-based architectural project planning. Thus, the influence of water on the character of architecture is understood not only as a shaper of the landscape, but also directly as a tool of architectural design. By looking at different urban scales and different typologies, from the city and industrial developments to small huts, the long-term project generated a comprehensive understanding of the uniqueness of each context studied. It was possible to generate building designs that approached the manifold facets of water and at the same time enabled new interpretations that went beyond this. Subsequently, the findings of the first research phase were analysed in greater depth from specific thematic perspectives. The strip remained the primary methodological tool – a strip that is understood as a section of a far more comprehensive area in the territorial infinity, but was geographically and thus culturally precisely rooted.

[1] The term palimpsest is derived from Greek *palimpsēstos*, from *palin*, "again", and *psēstos*, "rubbed smooth". It describes a manuscript on which two or more successive texts have been written, each one being erased to make room for the next.

Photo by BECK Jürgen

THE JOINT STUDIOS

In summary, the joint studios with four topics were not set in stone from the beginning, but each topic built on the foundation and experience of the previous topic. We started on stable and common grounds and then moved into differences and diversities. Based on the findings from the research semester, we started the first topic of "Danger", because the relationship between water and hazard is a fundamental subject. Without understanding the existing and potential dangers in the two beautiful lakes, we cannot touch upon the essence of the subject. Through the study of hazard maps, we realised that the current strategy towards natural hazards is rather technical and isolated from people's everyday lives. The architectural approach should not be one of confronting hazards head-on, but of skillfully submitting to and coexisting with them. Danger and survival are deeply related. The topic of "Beauty" arose from danger, and in the Lake Lucerne area we were looking for hidden beauty from the perspective of space and used it as the starting point for architectural design. On Lake Biwa, we examined the significance and development potential of classical beauty in the real world from the perspective of time. While studying the topic of beauty, no one anticipated that the world would be transformed due to the Covid pandemic, when people were kept apart from each other. However, the communication between the two universities did not stop. When we could not visit each other, we met online and developed diverse digital methods to do joint research and design. The third topic, "Commons", developed directly from this situation. It allowed us to think fundamentally about our relationship with the world. We were wondering how we could, through architectural research, bring together the common values and use architectural design as a creative problem-solving approach to lead the way to plausible visions. Finally, "Eternity" as the fourth topic evolved from this. Eternity led us to return to the origin of life and question ourselves on how to rebuild awareness of life and explore a sustainable future for the world in a material and immaterial way. One Water – Four Views[2] of Danger, Beauty, Commons and Eternity represents our entire five-year research project.

The environmental and ecological importance of the project has been present throughout our five-year programme. As final presentation, architectural models are not the bigger the better. We were very consious of the use and recycling of materials and energy. Physical "suitcase" models on individual scales are part of the semester assignment. They were to adopt the airplane hand baggage size to permit easy exchange and exhibition for the two universities. This is also a philosophy that we have learned from the Swiss and Japanese cultures in our projects, i.e. compactness, preciseness, adaptability and changeability, comparable to water.

[2] 山水经 Sansuikyō, Mountains and Waters Sutra, a masterpiece of poetry and insight from Eihei Dōgen, the 13th-century founder of the Sōtō school of Zen.

Marcel Duchamp, *Box in a Valise (From or by Marcel Duchamp or Rrose Sélavy)*, 1935–1941

YOON Solhae
Bus stop, Kusatsu

OWENS Kate
Capturing the forest, Seelisberg

SHABO Gabriela
Fish restaurant, Brunnen

PINELLI Manuele
Infrastructure, Ōtsu

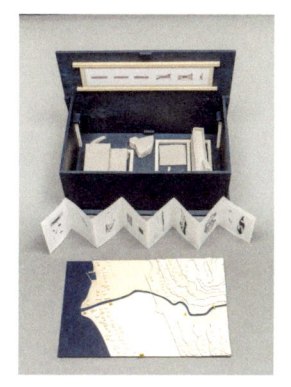

FURRER Juliana
Pottery Workshop, Ōtsu

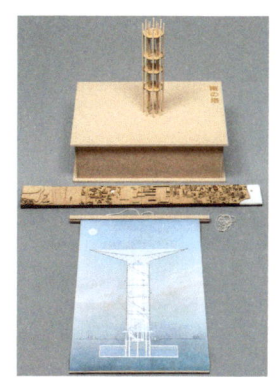

WENNER Liliane
Rain tower, Katata

PURKIS Roisin Elizabeth
The Roost, Vitznau

HERGER Thomas
Highway hostel, Hira

VICENCIO Maria Emelyn
Student Housing, Horw

Students

Autumn 2018

AKIMOTO Yumi
BEKCIC Predrag
DEL RÍO ARES André
GUIGNARD Gilles
HARA Hiroyuki
HUSTINX Charlotte
IMANISHI Shiori
ISLAMAJ Shehrie
JENNI Nico
MEIER Guilherme
MISAGHI Bejan
MUNETA Nana
MURAVLJOV Ruzica
OLIVELLA CIRICI Jordi
ROTH Dominic
SAKAMOTO Masako
SCHWEIZER Philip
SHABO Gabriela
SIMIĆ Ivan
SUN Meng
TAKAFUJI Tomoo
YAMADE Chika
YAMAGUCHI Daiki

Spring 2019

AMSTAD Ana Bela
BÜCHEL Larissa
DI FLAVIO Marco
FUKUI Masayuki
KARL Oliver
KAWABE Ayako
KAWAHATA Jun
KESSLER Remo
NEKOLNA Alena
NISHITSUJI Honami
ONOE Atsushi
OTHMAN Afifah
SAKAKI Kazusa
SHALA Milot
SIMIĆ Ivan
SUGAWARA Michiko
SUMITOMO Mahoko
SUZUKI Toru
TSUJITA Maki
WUST Max
ZHANG Yue

Autumn 2019

ACKERMANN Sophie
BADER Jennifer
BEKCIC Predrag
CHEN Kai
CULCAY Belen
D'HAENEN Silke
DE SMET Jan-Karl

FURRER Juliana
GUGGER Florian
HARADE Kanta
INABA Kanade
KOUNITZKY Helena
LUCKHARDT Christina
MARTINEZ Manuel
NOMURA Kano
PETRACCA Francesco
PINELLI Manuele
RUGGERI Leonardo
SAKAMOTO Asato
SAKUMA Kaori
SHIOZAKI Kyoko
THELEN Niklas
UEBAYASHI Yoshiya
WACKER Pascal
ZAPPA Elisa

Spring 2020

AL ZAMIL Al Jawharah
AMSTAD Ana Bela
CASINO LOZANO Maria
CULCAY Belen
D'HAENEN Silke
DANDEKAR Darakhsha
DE SMET Jan-Karl
FURRER Juliana
GJINAJ Egzon
GRODTKE Noemi Elise
ITO Souichiro
JO Tsuyu
KALTENBACH Larissa
KANAZAWA Misato
MASUDA Junpei
MULLE Jana
NOMURA Ryohei
ODAKA Ryo
OKINO Jun
PINELLI Manuele
TAKEDA Aya
YOSHIMURA Moeri
ZAPPA Elisa

Autumn 2020

ALEN MENDES Cristina
ANTONINI Nicola
BAER Rebecca
BRAUN Xenia
DE ALMEIDA Sara
DEGUCHI Kento
ELIZAROVA Vlada
GHODKI Aboli
HERGER Thomas
HOSSEINIAN Golnar
KANAZAWA Misato
KOJIMA Hiroki
KOTTATHU Christian
FUKAYA Mao

MASUDA Junpei
MÜLLER Dario
PACHERA Julia
POCHKAENKO Irina
PURKIS Roisin Elizabeth
TAKEDA Aya
TANAKA Yu
TSCHUPPERT Simon
WEIBEL Werner
WENNER Liliane
YOSHIMURA Moeri

Spring 2021

BAER Rebecca
BAKIR Zouhir
DELLO IOIO Giovanni
FOTHERINGHAM Hannah
HAMAIE Mari
HIROSE Ryotaro
HORSTHEMKE Hilke
JOHANSSON Lisa
OUNIBOS Shane
NANAO Yoko
POCHKAENKO Irina
PURKIS Roisin Elizabeth
REDWOOD Joe
SHABO Gabriela
SHIBAMURA Yusa
TOYAMA Daiki
VICENCIO Maria Emy
WATANABE Kodai
YAMAGIWA Asaka
YANENKO Oleksandr
YOON Solhae
ZAREI Negar

Autumn 2021

DELFOSSE Lukas
FURTER Tobias
JABBOURI Ichrake
KAWASHIMA Fumiya
LI Shuhui
JOHANSSON Lisa
NAKAGAWA Takahisa
NARITA Haruka
PAVLIŠTA Jindřich
ROBIN RODRIGUEZ Laura
RUSHITI Gëzim
SHEGAY Alina
SIMIĆ Ivan
TABATA Ko
TAKEDA Akane
TOYAMA Daiki
TSCHOPP Mario
YAMAGIWA Asaka
YANAGISAWA Daichi
YOON Solhae
ZEJNULLAHU Amir

Spring 2022

BJØRNEVIK Sara
DELFOSSE Lukas
IKENARI Takahiro
IMAHASHI Keigo
KAWASAKI Ren
LUBISHTANI Art
MATSUI Natsu
NAITOU Sari
NAKAI Sotaro
NAKAO Taichi
OMURO Arata
OWENS Kate
PREUSS Jan
ROMA GÓMEZ Blanca
SHEGAY Alina
SHIMIZU Natsumi
YAMAMOTO Saika
YANG Huangyu
YOON Solhae
ZEJNULLAHU Amir
ZHANG Yicong

Autumn 2022

BAYARAA Maral
HIROSE Ryotaro
HORSTHEMKE Hilke
IKENARI Takahiro
KAWAKAMI Kota
KURISU Shota
LUBISHTANI Art
MALCINOVIC Anel
NIMURA Azuki
OKADA Tsukuru
RUSHITI Rinor
SHEGAY Alina
TAKAYOSHI Kaito

Tutors

ARAGÜEZ Marcela
DEON Luca
DUSSEILER Yves
GEISSBÜHLER Dieter
KÄFERSTEIN Joahnnes
KIMURA Hiroyuki
KINOSHITA Masahiro
MOLO Ludovica
ROSSMAIER Lando
SEIFERT Annika
SUN BUSCHOR Mulan
TEUTSCH Uwe
WETTSTEIN Felix

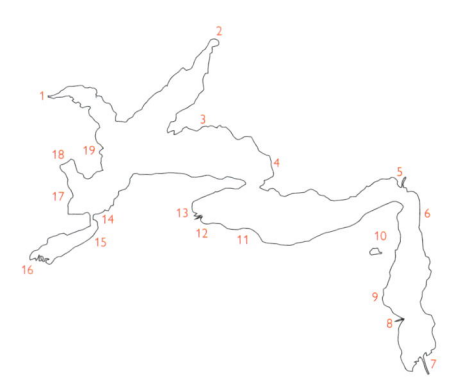

1 Lucerne
2 Küssnacht
3 Weggis
4 Vitznau
5 Brunnen
6 Morschach
7 Flüelen
8 Isleten
9 Bauen
10 Seelisberg
11 Beckenried
12 Buochs
13 Ennetbürgen
14 Stansstad
15 Rotzloch
16 Alpnachstad
17 Hergiswil
18 Horw
19 St. Niklausen

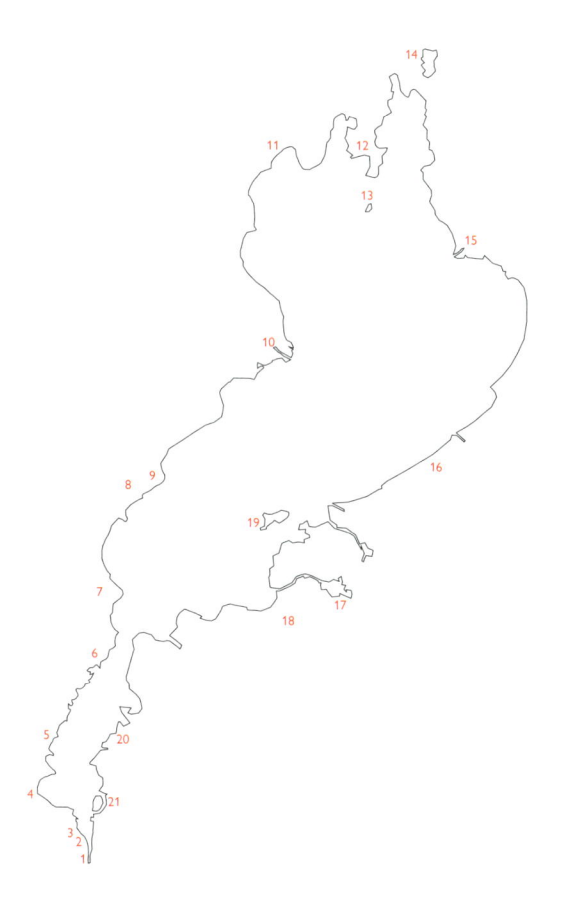

1 Seta
2 Ishiyama
3 Awazu
4 Miidera
5 Karasaki
6 Katata
7 Ōtsu
8 Hira
9 Ōmi-Maiko
10 Takashima
11 Makino
12 Sugaura
13 Chikubushima
14 Yogoko
15 Nagahama
16 Kojinyama
17 Nishinoko
18 Ōmihachiman
19 Okishima
20 Kusatsu
21 Yabase

Study trip of HSLU students, three-day Zen meditation at Lassalle Haus, Bad Schönbrunn, autumn 2021

Joint final review in Horw, spring 2023

HSLU students' arrival with suitcase models at Tokyo airport, spring 2023

Study trip of HSLU and KIT students to Ise Shrine, spring 2023

Exhibition in Horw, spring 2019

Neither the project "The Culture of Water" nor the book *Two Lakes* could have been undertaken without what we were able to learn from lectures, critiques, workshops and mentoring woven across time from 2018 to 2023 with the following experts and scholars:

ARAGÜEZ Marcela	Lecture, Japanese beauty – input/output, spring 2020
DE MOLFETTA Federico	Lecture and critique, Landscape metabolism, autumn 2022
GEISSBÜHLER Dieter	Lecture, Water and Productivity, spring 2021
	Lecture, Layers of Lake Lucerne with a focus on the Urnerbecken, spring 2022
DUSSEILER Yves	Lecture, Eternity with stone, spring 2022
HELFREICH Silke	Lecture, Free, Fair and Alive – The Insurgent Power of the Commons, spring 2021
HOPE Strode	Lecture and critique, Landscape metabolism, autumn 2022
HORAT Heinz	Lecture, Lake Lucerne – Architecture, Forms of Living, Landscape Condition, spring 2020
IDO Misato	Lecture, Japanese Beauty and Eight Views, autumn 2020
INOUE Miyuki	Guest critique, autumn 2022
JASPER Adam	Lecture, Water Management Bali, autumn 2022
JOANELLY Tibor	Lecture, Beauty, spring 2020
KIMURA Hiroyuki	Lecture, Is beauty (of a building) autonomous? spring 2020
	Lecutre, The Culture of Water, Asia Pacific Architecture Festival 2022
KINOSHITA Masahiro	Lecture, Optimised architecture, spring 2020
KOHLHAMMER Thomas	Lecture, Structure and Beauty, spring 2020
KOHTE Susanne	Lecture, autumn 2018
LEMBKE Jürgen Jian	Workshop on Zen meditation, autumn 2021
MARTINEZ-CAÑAVATE Celina	Lecture, Touch wood, autumn 2022
NAKAYAMA Rie	Lecture, Traditional techniques in maintaining Japanese wooden architecture, spring 2023
OHASHI Karin	Lecture, Perfection and Imperfection – A draft on Japanese aesthetic, autumn 2020
	Ikebana workshop, autumn 2020
ONO Yoshiro	Mentor
SCHMID Christian	Lecture, City network of central Switzerland, spring 2021
SCHULZ Uwe	Mentor
SCHWYZER-MUKAI Yumi	Lecture, Ritual in Japan, autumn 2021
STEINECK Raji C.	Lecture, Water in historic Japanese culture, autumn 2019
SUN BUSCHOR Mulan	Lecture, Programme and beauty, spring 2020
	Chado workshop – Japanese tea ceremony, autumn 2020
	Lecutre, The Culture of Water, Asia Pacific Architecture Festival 2022
TANE Tsuyoshi	Lecture, Archaeology of the future, autumn 2020
TEUTSCH Uwe	Structural expert to the design studio
THOMSEN Chikako Fukami	Lecture and calligraphy workshop, autumn 2020
THOMSEN Hans Bjarne	Lecture, Eight Views of Ōmi, autumn 2020,
	Lecture, The Past and Present of Japanese Rituals and Common Life, autumn 2021
TSUDA Kazutoshi	Lecture, Water and architecture under the theme of Re-Metabolism: Stories of media art centre, Japanese garden, and thatched house, autumn 2022
VIRAY Erwin	Mentor
VON MOOS Stanislaus	Lecture, autumn 2018
	Lecture, Panorama, Development, Control – A Discovery of Lake Lucerne, spring 2021

INSTEAD OF AN EPILOGUE
エピローグの代わりに

KINOSHITA Masahiro

INSTEAD OF AN EPILOGUE

What were we trying to find by comparing the two lakes?

If architecture is the mediator between nature and people, its appearance is influenced by the place where it is located; thus, by researching the two lakes and their cultures we can see the characteristics of the architecture in each place.

So, when we think about architecture as a mediator between nature and people, what kind of approach can we take?

The selected themes that we explored were "Water and Danger", "Water and Beauty", "Water and Commons" and "Water and Eternity".

And these aspects are directly related to the fundamental elements of architecture: "strength, function and beauty". Thinking about the two lakes was synonymous with thinking about architecture.

Architecture is a mediator between nature and people. Therefore, if the natural environment changes, or if the way people live changes, architecture will subsequently also change, or rather, it must change, or else it can no longer be a mediator. So, what potential for change could we find in this project?

In our discussion of "Water and Danger", we realised that architecture serves not only as a shelter from natural disasters, but also as a medium to forewarn us of danger. Architecture as shelter, however, separates people from nature, to avoid danger. It can be said that the students in their designs were exploring ways to respond to danger while retaining the experience of the rich beauty of nature.

THELEN Niklas: In the riverbed, Oya River, Ōtsu

The following approach, "Water and Beauty", investigated the beauty of nature. If beauty in its most perfect state is undisturbed nature in its natural state, then it would be better if neither people nor architecture were involved. However, when nature and people come together through architecture, there is also sure to be beauty. We sought to find such beauty. The way in which beauty exists differs depending on whether there is little or a lot of human involvement in each lake. By changing our perspective and reconstructing the relationship between the two, we set out to prove that human involvement creates new beauty.

Photo by BECK Jürgen

Having realised that human relationships create new forms of beauty, we then decided to focus on these relationships and think about the commons. This was the third theme, "Water and Commons". How can commons be formed? What kind of architecture is possible when there are trustworthy commons, and what kind of environment is mediated by such architecture? Thinking about these questions can result in a new form of architecture.

woodblockprint by ito shinsui: mount hira | from 8 views of omi | 1917

HERGER Thomas: Evening snow on Hira Mountains

While thinking about "danger", "beauty" and "commons", I was always conscious of "time". When we discussed "danger", we considered how to deal with the difference between "ordinary" time and "extraordinary" time, such as during a disaster. When we discussed "beauty", we understood the need to consider time, such as "beauty is in the moment" and "beauty is cultivated over a long period of time". And when we discussed "commons", we were made to think about its sustainability.

Based on such thinking about time, the next topic we took up was "Water and Eternity".

Thinking about eternity is also to think about sustainability. How does a person with a finite lifespan achieve eternity? Can the natural environment remain unchanged and sustainable? These questions themselves are eternal themes. And the difference in the two lakes manifests itself as a difference in time. The difference between eternal existence and the eternal mechanism is reflected in the different architectural manifestations. Both appearances are maintained in form, but the way in which the form is maintained is different. While stone remains the same stone forever, wood is replaced by new wood.

This joint studio, which took on four themes from the perspective of our relationship with water, was an attempt to consider the future of architecture. The results of this work will surely be the prelude to a new kind of architecture.

YOON Solhae:
Central Barter Market

KINOSHITA Masahiro:
A common grave in Fukuoka
Photo by NAKAMURA Kai

Murasaki Shikibu: *The Tale of Genji*, published before 1021, Japan

Garrett Hardin: "The Tragedy of the Commons". In: *Science*. Vol. 162, Issue 3859, 1968, p. 1243–1248

Edmund Burke: *A Philosophical Enquiry into the Origin of our Ideas of the Sublime and Beautiful*, London 1757

William Forster Lloyd: *Two Lectures on the Checks to Population*, Oxford 1833

Elinor Ostrom: *Governing the Commons. The Evolution of Institutions for Collective Action*, Cambridge 1990

Stanislaus von Moos: *Nicht Disneyland und andere Aufsätze über Modernität und Nostalgie*, Zurich 2004

Roger Diener / Jacques Herzog / Marcel Meili / Pierre de Meuron / Christian Schmid, *Switzerland – an Urban Portrait*, ETH Studio Basel 2005

Trudy Dixon / Suzuki Shunryu: *Zen Mind, Beginner's Mind*, Boulder, CO 2006

Bruno Latour: *Facing Gaia. Eight Lectures on the New Climatic Regime*, trans. Catherine Porter, Cambridge 2017

François Jullien: *Living off Landscape; or, The Unthought-Of in Reason*, trans. Pedro Rodríguez, Lanham, 2018

Ono Yoshiro, *Water System in the Capital of Kyoto*, SHIBUNKAKU CO., LTD., 2015

Okumura Shohaku with contributions by Carl Bielefeldt, Gary Snyder, Issho Fujita and Shodo Spring: *The Mountains and Waters Sutra. A Practitioner's Guide to Dogen's "Sansuikyo"*, Somerville, MA 2018

Tane Tsuyoshi: *Archaeology of the Future*, Tokyo 2018

David Bollier / Silke Helfrich: *Free, Fair, and Alive: The Insurgent Power of the Commons*, Gabriola Island, BC 2019

Angelika Juppien / Franziska Winterberger/ Richard Zemp: *Innovative Wohnformen. Kontext, Typologien und Konsequenzen*, CCTP, Lucerne University of Applied Sciences (HSLU) 2019

Hartmut Rosa: *Resonanz. Eine Soziologie der Weltbeziehung*, Berlin 2019

Tahara Yukio / Kasahara Kazuto / Rie Nakayama (Eds.)xxxxx [Conservation and Regeneration Design of Buildings and Cities. For the Rich Succession of Modern Cultural Heritage], Tokyo 2019

Tibor Joanelly: *Shinoharistics. An Essay about a House*, Zurich 2020

Han Byung-Chul: *The Disappearance of Rituals. A Topology of the Present*, trans. Daniel Steuer, Cambridge 2021

Emanuele Coccia: *Metamorphoses, trans. Robin Mackay*, Cambridge and Oxford 2021

Karin Ohashi / Lando Rossmaier (Eds.): *Feine Fassaden – Tektonik Schweizer Stadthäuser*, Lucerne 2022

Sergio Risalti / Corinna Thierolf / Gerhard Wolf: *Wolfgang Laib in Florence*, Munich 2022

Carla Ferrer / Thomas Hildebrand / Celina Martinez-Cañavate: *Touch Wood*, Zurich 2023

Judith Rauser / Hans Bjarne Thomsen: *Made in Japan: Farbholzschnitte von Hiroshige, Kunisada und Hokusai*, Berlin 2024

P. 6–19: Photos of Lake Lucerne by BECK Jürgen
P. 20–21: Handdrawn maps of Lake Lucerne and Lake Biwa by TSCHOPP Mario
P. 22–35: Photos of Lake Biwa by TAKANO Tomomi

P. 36: Photo by BECK Jürgen
P. 38–39: Photos by KÄFERSTEIN Johannes
P. 40: *Atlas der Schweiz von Meyer, Weiss und Müller, 1796–1802* (excerpt from sheet no. 7). This was the first modern atlas of Switzerland, inspired by General Pfyffer's relief of primeval Switzerland
P. 41: The Ino map of Japan at scale 1:36,000 was created by INO Tadataka as a set of 214 sheets during 1800–1821. This map with a detailed coastal survey is also known as 大日本沿海輿地全図 Dai Nihon enkai yochi zenzu, or Inō Daizu. The section around Lake Biwa shown here was produced by the editorial team for this publication, from an incomplete set of Ino maps from the United States Library of Congress (coloured reproduction) held by the Geospatial Information Authority of Japan (GSI), combining it with another incomplete set of Ino maps held by Hydrographic and Oceanographic Department of Japan Coast Guard (reproduced and colour-restored by the GSI with permission). The section comprises parts of sheets Nos. 188, 121, 122, 125, 126, 129 and 133. It has been scaled according to page size for this publication. Original data from GSI Historical Map Collection: https://kochizu.gsi.go.jp/inouzu

P. 42: Photo by BECK Jürgen
P. 43, 44, 48, 52, 58, 62, 68, 72, 80: Diagram by SUN BUSCHOR Mulan
45: Hazard map of Beckenried, ©swisstopo
P. 46: Student project by SAKAKI Kazusa; student project by OTHMAN Afifah
P. 47: *Isle of the Dead,* Basel version, Arnold Böcklin, 1880; student project by WUST Max
P. 50: Student project by UEBAYASHI Yoshiya; student project by NOMURA Kano
P. 51: Student project by MARTINEZ Manuel
P. 53: Student project by MULLE Jana
P. 55: Student project by AL ZAMIL Al Jawharah
P. 57: Student project by OKINO Jun
P. 59: Ukiyo-e by Utagawa Hiroshige; student project by BAER Rebecca; Ukiyo-e by Utagawa Hiroshige; student project by KOJIMA Hiroki
P. 61: Ukiyo-e by Utagawa Hiroshige; student project by WEIBEL Werner; Ukiyo-e by Utagawa Hiroshige; KANAZAWA Misato
P. 63: Photo by Roland Zumbuehl
P. 64: Photo by Piotr Metelski
P. 66: Student project by PURKIS Róisín Elizabeth
P. 67: Student project by BAER Rebecca
P. 70: Part of the Murasaki Shikibu Diary Emaki, Gotoh edition. color and ink on paper, 21cm height; 十輪院正面の明障子 by Ktmchi, 2016; student project by KAWASHIMA Fumiya
P. 71: Student project by FURTER Tobias
P. 73: Photo by ROSSMAIER Lando, Kunsthaus Zurich, 2020
P. 76: Student project by NAITOU Sari
P. 79: Student project by ROMA GÓMEZ Blanca
P. 81: Photo of Lake Lucerne by SUN BUSCHOR Mulan, 2024
P. 82: Photo by SUN BUSCHOR Mulan, Wolfgang Laib's exhibition in Bündner Kunstmuseum Chur, 2022
P. 83: Student project by HAMAIE Mari
P. 85: Student project by SHEGAY Alina, photo by KÄCH Markus; photography by Werner Bischof, Waterdipper at the tea ceremony, Kyoto, 1951, Modern gelatin silver print (estate print), 35.7 × 44 cm, IBASHO
P. 86: Photo by BECK Jürgen
P. 92: *The Autumn Full Moon at Ishiyama,* Utagawa Hiroshige, ca. 1832, https://www.metmuseum.org/art/collection/search/56898
P. 93: *Vierwaldstättersee – Lake Lucerne* by Willy F. Burger, 1941, http://adikaelin.ch/wp-content/uploads/Burger_340.jpg

P. 94: Photo by BECK Jürgen
P. 96: 2025 Artists Rights Society (ARS), New York / ADAGP, Paris / Estate of Marcel Duchamp
P. 97: Suitcases photography by KÄCH Markus
P. 99: Sites around Lake Lucerne and Lake Biwa, Diagram by SUN BUSCHOR Mulan
P. 100: Photos from top left to bottom right by SIMIĆ Ivan, DUSSEILLER Yves, passersby, LIU Yuxia, KÄCH Markus
P. 102: Photo by BECK Jürgen
P. 104: Student project by HERGER Thomas
P. 105: Student project by YOON Solhae; Project by KINOSHITA Masahiro, Photo by NAKAMURA Kai

EDITORS

GEISSBÜHLER Dieter graduated as architect from the ETH in Zurich. Teaching at the ETH in Zurich and from 2000 to 2020 as Professor at the Lucerne University of Applied Sciences and Arts – Engineering & Architecture, heading the studio "Architecture & Material". Currently he is partner in the firm Geissbühler Venschott Architekten in Luzern. He is working as a designer and consultant and he also writes about issues of contemporary architecture.

KÄFERSTEIN Johannes graduated as architect from the ETH in Zurich. He was head of the Institute of Architecture at the Lucerne University of Applied Sciences and Arts – Engineering & Architecture from 2008 to 2024, he was President of the Architecture Council of Switzerland and is currently the President of the Center Architecture Zurich (ZAZ). He is the founder and co-owner of Käferstein & Meister Architects in Zurich.

KIMURA Hiroyuki was project professor at Kyoto Institute of Technology from 2019 to 2024. He graduated as an architect from the University of Tokyo and EPFL in Laussane. From 1999 to 2017 he worked as an architect at Diener & Diener Architekten in Basel. He is a founding director of Machi Mura Studio in Tokyo.

KINOSHITA Masahiro was born in Shiga, Japan. He graduated from Kyoto Institute of Technology and founded KINO architects in 2007. His focus is on designing buildings that address social issues, including nurseries, libraries and offices. His philosophy, "fostering a sustainable society through architecture", aims at creating spaces that rejuvenate nature and urban communities. He began teaching at Kyoto Institute of Technology in 2014, became an associate professor in 2021, and was a visiting researcher at ETH Zurich in 2016, focusing on sustainable architectural design.

SUN BUSCHOR Mulan is project leader of the Culture of Water. She was born and grew up in Tianjin, China and graduated as an architect from the ETH in Zurich in 2010. From 2015 to 2024, she taught Architectural Research and Design at the Lucerne University of Applied Sciences and Arts, ETH Zurich and Tianjin University. She is founder and co-owner of SML Architektur in Zurich. She is also a tea master and senior lecturer of Japanese Way of Tea, Urasenke Tea School.

AUTHORS

DEON Luca headed the studio "Architecture & Energy" at the HSLU from 2003 to 2023 and collaborated with the Culture of Water from autumn semester 2020 to spring semester 2021. He is the principal of the architecture office DEON AG in Lucerne.

MOLO Ludovica heads the studio "Architecture & Structure" at the HSLU and collaborated with the Culture of Water from autumn semester 2019 to spring semester 2020. She is the director of i2a Istituto Internazionale di Architettura and partner of studio we architecture in Lugano.

ROSSMAIER Lando headed the studio "Architecture & Material" at the HSLU from 2020 to 2023 (2013–2023 at the HSLU T&A) and collaborated with the Culture of Water from autumn semester 2021 to spring semester 2022. He is the principal of Atelier Lando Rossmaier in Ennenda.

SEIFERT Annika headed the studio "Architecture & Energy" at the HSLU from 2017 to 2024 and collaborated with the Culture of Water from autumn semester 2020 to spring semester 2021. She currently holds the chair of Climate Responsive Architecture at University of Stuttgart and practices with APC Architects, Dar es Salaam, Tanzania.

THOMSEN Hans Bjarne is a professor at the Institute of Art History at the University of Zurich. In 2019, he was awarded "The Order of the Rising Sun, Gold Rays with Rosette" from imperial orders by the Japanese government.

WETTSTEIN Felix heads the studio "Architecture & Structure" at the HSLU and collaborated with the Culture of Water from the autumn semester 2019 to the spring semester 2020. He is principal of studio we architecture in Lugano.

PHOTOGRAPHERS

BECK Jürgen lives and works in Zurich. His publications were shown at the Swiss Art Awards, Kunsthalle Luzern, Ditch Projects, New Toni and Last Tango. He was a fellow at the Cité Internationale des Arts Paris and will be an artist in residence at the Bauhaus Residency programme Dessau in 2025.

TAKANO Tomomi creates photos and videos with architects, designers and artists based in Kyoto. She also creates artworks to explore alternative ways of representation using her unique photographic process.

We would like to express our sincerest gratitude and deepest appreciation to the following institutions and sponsoring companies whose financial support contributed significantly to the publication of this book. Their cultural commitment enables a fruitful and friendly cooperation of the culture and education exchange between Switzerland and Japan.

HSLU Foundation
Die Stiftung der Hochschule Luzern

ERNST GÖHNER STIFTUNG

Fondation
Sakae Stünzi

日本・スイス国交樹立記念
Anniversary of Diplomatic Relations
between Japan and Switzerland

TWO LAKES ふたつのみずうみ
Lake Lucerne and Lake Biwa:
A Comparative Study on the Culture of Water

Laboratorium Switzerland – Japan
Hochschule Luzern – Technik & Architektur
Kyoto Institute of Technology – KYOTO Design Lab

Editors and publication concept: GEISSBÜHLER Dieter,
KÄFERSTEIN Johannes, KIMURA Hiroyuki, KINOSHITA Masahiro,
SUN BUSCHOR Mulan
Project management: SUN BUSCHOR Mulan
Text contributions: DEON Luca, GEISSBÜHLER Dieter, KÄFERSTEIN
Johannes, KIMURA Hiroyuki, KINOSHITA Masahiro, MOLO Ludovica,
ROSSMAIER Lando, SEIFERT Annika, SUN BUSCHOR Mulan,
THOMSEN Hans Bjarne, WETTSTEIN Felix
Proofreading: BLACKADDER KÄFERSTEIN Annie
Copy editing: STEIN Ria
Redesign: BKVK, Basel – Beat Keusch, Vanessa Serrano
Graphic design: Quart Verlag Luzern
Lithos: Rica Egger, Printeria, Lucerne
Printing: DZA Druckerei zu Altenburg GmbH

Product safety
Responsible person pursuant to EU Regulation 2023/988 (GPSR):
GVA Gemeinsame Verlagsauslieferung Göttingen GmbH & Co. KG
Post Box 2021
37010 Göttingen
Germany
info@gva-verlage.de
T +49 551 384 200 0
www.gva-verlage.dee

Quart Verlag GmbH
Denkmalstrasse 2, CH-6006 Luzern
books@quart.ch, T +41 41 420 20 82, www.quart.ch

LABORATORIUM

Laboratorium: A study environment in which to reflect, but above all
to work and experiment. It is not just for testing, but also for presenting
ideas and theories, in brief – a place of research. Because *laborare*
not only means "to work", but also "to make an effort", it is therefore
an activity with an open end.

books@quart.ch, www.quart.ch